T0194132

Finding Brave

MY JOURNEY FROM A
LIFE *of* FEAR TO ONE *of* HOPE

Jamie Taylor

WESTBOW
PRESS®
A DIVISION OF THOMAS NELSON
& ZONDERVAN

WestBow Press books may be ordered through booksellers or by contacting:

WestBow Press
A Division of Thomas Nelson & Zondervan
1663 Liberty Drive
Bloomington, IN 47403
www.westbowpress.com
1 (866) 928-1240

ISBN: 978-1-9736-2774-6 (sc)
ISBN: 978-1-9736-2776-0 (hc)
ISBN: 978-1-9736-2775-3 (e)

Library of Congress Control Number: 2018905498

Print information available on the last page.

WestBow Press rev. date: 05/08/2018

For Brian, who has walked beside me on this journey - through the hardest days and the darkest nights. I love you.

Contents

Introduction ix

1. Baby Blues 1
2. The Assured Agoraphobic 11
3. Driving Distressed 21
4. The Panicked Pastor's Wife 31
5. Nursery Nightmares 43
6. Medicine, Marriage & Milestones 53
7. The Scary Stage 69
8. Stepping out of Safety to Serve 81
9. Walking with Women 93
10. When Callings Collide 105
11. Joy in the Journey 119
12. Power over Paralysis 129

Afterword 135
Acknowledgements 141
Verses for Hope & Healing 143
Resources 147

Contents

Introduction

This isn't the book I dreamed about writing when I was young.

In fact, when I first sat down to begin writing my experience with anxiety and depression; I didn't have a fixed goal in mind. I was simply aware that the words needed to fill a page. My story needed to be shared, even if it was just with a small group of friends. I felt drawn to share what I have gone through up to this point because I wish I could have heard these words from someone during my darkest days. I needed to hear I wasn't alone.

It can be difficult when writing a book like this, because there already are so many good resources out there on mental health. I can't tell you how many books I have seen advertised just this year that promise to help us break out of our fears and live a victorious life. Just so you know, I'm not reinventing the wheel. This is not a self-help book, and it's not my autobiography. This is me sharing my story and hoping you are inspired and challenged by the lessons God has taught me. I've been tempted to shrink back from being vulnerable because I don't have all the answers.

This short summary of my experience took over two years to write down. Part of the reason for that is because I was still very much in process (I believe I will always be "in process"). Healing from emotional pain does not happen overnight. In my experience, I've come across no one who found perfection in their lifetime.

There are two things that I want to tell you before you read this book. The first is that mental health crises' are very real experiences. Let me assure you from the onset that people are typically not being "dramatic" when they tell you they deal with panic disorder, anxiety or depression. I used to think these kinds of issues weren't that big of a deal. "People just need to get a grip," I would think to myself. "It can't be that bad." How very wrong I was. If someone in your life is going through an emotional hurdle, the best thing you can do for them in the beginning is to *believe them*. Assure them they aren't crazy. Help them on the path to their healing. And, if that person who needs healing is you, I want to assure you that you are not alone in the struggle. My hope for you is that you will stop running away from the difficult journey, and will lean into it instead. You need a life more abundant. You weren't made for half-cup living.

Secondly, I want you to understand that perfection is not the goal. Healing doesn't mean that you won't feel scared or frustrated or worried. It won't mean you will always walk through each day with a cool, calm attitude. Life has mountains and valleys, and you will continue to experience those. The majority of people I talk to aren't interested in the kind of self-help that comes off as fake and unrealistic. Instagram worthy perfection is not where most of us live. We feel deep hurts and cry real tears. (Oh, and our sink has dirty dishes in it every single day).

The goal in my writing will never be to paint a picture of wholeness on earth, because it doesn't exist. We were created for eternity, and we aren't there yet. However, we can reach a place of meaning where heaven comes down to meet us in our weaknesses. A place of freedom and hope in which we live the life we were created to. I want that for you. I want you to be free.

I lived for ten years with physical and mental chains around my body. I felt an overwhelming urgency to run, and yet my feet were enveloped in quicksand. I wasn't sure I would ever feel "normal" again.

Normal is defined by the Merriam Webster dictionary as "not deviating from a norm, rule, or principle." Another description is "conforming to a type, standard, or regular pattern." One definition even goes so far as to say, "free from mental illness: mentally sound."

My question in response to this information is this, "If so many people struggle with fear, anxiety, and depression, what does that say about our concept of normalcy?"

Why is it that so many of us can't seem to break free to live what we envision as a "normal" life?

I believe that one of the reasons it took me so long to find healing is because of the stigma attached to mental health concerns. I didn't want a label. I didn't want sympathy. I didn't want to be different. So, instead, I lived my anxiety out as secretly as I could. My body suffered. My family suffered. And, my mind suffered to such a great extent, that I became physically sick as a result.

Every human will be faced with periods of pain, moments of fear and seasons of emotional ups and downs. That is the normal part of life. What isn't normal however, is what I experienced for a ten year period of my life. I lived a life of preoccupation with worry, fear, and distress. I was terrified on a daily basis. I was bound with chains that were not easily broken.

This is my story of deliverance.

It is my prayer that you find freedom from your chains of fear and anxiety, and that this book could be instrumental in helping you or someone you love further along that path.

"In my experience, the words 'now just calm down' almost inevitably have the opposite effect on the person you are speaking to."

- Elyn R. Saks

1

Baby Blues

The Starting Point

Most of us have heard of the possibility of something called the "baby blues." Pregnancy and childbirth have a way of changing the course of a woman's inclination toward normalcy. This was the case in my experience.

I've always been a firm believer in the power of multitasking. And it just so happened my first child was born in the middle of one of my greatest multitasking periods. I was graduating from nursing school, taking my state boards, and juggling side jobs right before our eldest made her grand entrance. I found I had great difficulty cultivating coping mechanisms. The baby blues turned me into a person I couldn't hope to recognize.

First, a new mom is subject to a great deal of pressure. Everything has to be just right. She must feed the baby at the proper time and use the proper method. According to some camps, she must sleep train her child beginning at birth. According to others, she must allow that child to sleep next to her until close to his or her eighteenth birthday. Oh, and don't get me started on immunizations! More stress has been caused by that debate than almost anything. Even though that is said in jest, a great variety in parenting standards are typically conveyed to new parents.

How is one to sort them out? I perused books and magazine articles, and talked to countless people about their particular methods. I became a student of proper parenting. After consulting a great number of witnesses, I realized I now had another problem. I had so many thoughts about the art of parenting but truly no idea where to begin with any of them.

To be completely honest, I had a great deal of expectations for my first childbirth experience and the days that followed. I told friends about the plans I had for the proper care and feeding of my child. I knew what was best for babies, and I couldn't believe any mom would deprive her children of their God-given right— breast milk! I would *never* be one of "those moms" who embraced convenience over the correct method of nutrition. I beg you, dear reader, to offer me grace as I had a great deal to learn!

Little did I know that complications after birth and the repercussions that followed would hinder that precious commodity I held so dear. I found myself at the end of two weeks with a screaming, starving newborn, and no answers to the questions I asked. How could I be failing in the simplest of tasks? I couldn't even keep a baby healthy with what I considered the only way to feed my child. What would people think if I changed to a bottle with carefully crafted formula? What would I think of myself?

With a tear-stained pillow and what felt like a disappointing decision, I sacrificed my ego for the sake of my child. I was humbled. I felt like a failure. A fake. A fraud. Why had I been so hard on moms just like me? Why had I assumed I knew anything about their decisions? And why was it any of my business in the first place?

What I needed in those early days was for someone to look me in the eye and affirm that I was a good mom, even if I did things differently than others. I was keeping my sweet baby girl alive. But somehow that seemed inadequate because of the level of expectations I placed on myself.

I tell you this to let you in on the ground level of my struggle with control. When you feel you cannot control what should be the simplest of things, you imagine your world is spinning out of place. Little things become enormous obstacles in a mind determined to find perfection.

To make matters worse, I had just finished a degree in nursing. The medical field was something I had wanted to be part of my entire life. Imagine me, as a little girl, always playing the nurse, telling everyone around me that I would one day take care of real patients. Every dream of mine revolved around my desire to be the next Florence Nightingale. I was determined to heal the sick and hurting.

Suddenly, I was all grown up with the degree in hand, and it wasn't going so well. I experienced a tremendous amount of angst about what I should do coupled with the fact I wasn't cut out for my life's dream. Not only was I dealing with the repercussions of being enormously empathetic (we're talking pain in my body as I cared for my patients), I was crumbling under the pressure of being a new nurse. Frankly, I could not deal with the expectations. As much as

I loved caring for people, I struggled greatly with certain aspects of the job. I didn't handle stress well and couldn't imagine admitting I might not be suited for the one thing I always wanted to do. In my mind, I was a failure.

I found myself in an awkward position that felt terrifying. I was a new nurse who wasn't sure I could cut it in my job. And I was a new mom who wasn't sure I was capable as a mom. In the context of these momentous changes, I was about to enter a new reality.

The Panic Attack

While I wore many hats during this period, one of my favorite titles was caregiver. My husband, Brian, and I worked for an elderly woman, doing odd jobs and serving as her companion. The day of the attack started much like all the other ones with my newborn daughter and I going to work together. I had been asked to drive my sweet woman to her dentist appointment, and nothing could have prepared me for what was about to happen.

As we eased our way into the city traffic and came to a stop behind a line of waiting cars, I suddenly felt all the air leave my chest. I felt as if I couldn't take a deep breath. My head began to communicate confusion to the rest of my body. I looked to the left and the right, knowing I had to get off the road before I passed out. My heart beat at an insane speed, and the breaths I took were so rapid that even my thoughts couldn't keep up with them. I turned to the woman I cared for, willing her to look out for my well-being for a minute. "I have to stop," I told her. "I am not feeling well."

If only I had known then what I am very aware of now, I would have had a whole arsenal of helpful words to tell myself. But I had no coping mechanisms at that time and could not coach my scared brain into obedience. Frankly, I didn't even know what I was dealing with. More than that, I would never admit I was dealing with an anxiety attack because, in my ignorance, I believed only weak people dealt with that problem. I had much to learn about the complexity of the mind and how it can be hijacked without your consent.

After an embarrassing turn of events, which included my dad coming to help me drive home, I collapsed into an exhausted heap. Little did I know I had just lived through a whopper of a panic attack. Looking back, I can now see I had dealt with small anxiety attacks before this but brushed them off as circumstance or mood. It would be a long time before I would admit I had a problem that needed addressing. I was not then aware there might be lingering issues in the recesses of my mind needing to be coaxed out and discussed. Instead, I pushed away any idea that I had anxiety. I was just going through a "phase." I believed if I didn't tell anyone about it, it would go away.

This was almost laughable since I could hardly drive without hyperventilating. I wanted nothing to do with crowds, especially when it came to church. I remember one Sunday morning. We decided to have a ceremony during the service to dedicate our daughter to God. This involved the very vulnerable act of walking to the front of the church and standing for what felt like an exorbitant amount of time. I had never heard of the term "agoraphobia" (abnormal fear of being helpless in an embarrassing or unescapable situation that is characterized especially by the avoidance of open or public places), but the definition of that word is everything I felt. I held tightly to Brian's arm, willing myself to get through this moment of inescapable panic. At the time, I thought, *I just need to eat or something. My blood sugar might be low because I don't have a psychological problem. I will be fine.* I wanted to sit down, leave, or be anywhere but where I was at that moment.

Perhaps you have found yourself with a racing heart and mind, unsure of why a seemingly insignificant circumstance evokes such panic. I've been where you are, and I know you may feel like no one really sees or understands you. I get it. I see you. But more important, God sees you. He knows every intricate detail about your body. This is not some unexplainable phenomenon. I can promise that you can find healing from the unquenchable desire to run away.

The Endless Excuses

One coping mechanism I employed during this time was the delicate art of the perfect excuse. When you can't drive without serious fear, or time spent in a room with other people makes you physically ill, it becomes difficult to have a social life. While I had never been the life of the party, I certainly enjoyed times of frivolity with friends. But suddenly, I was faced with a real dilemma. I could let them in on my real crisis. Or I could pretend everything was fine and allow them to conclude I was perfect in every way.

Fearful seasons have a way of pushing us to the edge of dishonesty, don't they? We incorrectly assume that no one else is dealing with the fears that we are, and because of our desire to appear in control, we lie to ourselves and everyone else. Instead of opening ourselves up to a scenario where others empathize with our human weaknesses, we close up our hearts and minds to the idea of sharing our imperfect life.

Such was the case during the time of my acute panic. I had never lived a life that was characterized by a continual cold sweat and I knew that if my friends and family saw me in that light, I would lose all credibility as a calm, confident person. So when they would ask things of me that I could not handle without fear, I would craft the perfect excuse as to why I was unable to join them. I wonder now what some of them were thinking. How many of them knew what was actually going on, and just let me lie to cover up the real reason for my avoidance.

Let me stop at this point and tell you that it's okay to say no. The problem with the way I handled things is that I was dishonest with myself, and with others. Instead of saying, "I'm going through a tough time right now, and I just can't do that at this time," I would come up with an excuse to avoid telling the truth. I would even fabricate a clever commitment that would cause a conflict with the event being presented. Even if it was something as simple as my new baby, I would use any excuse to get out of facing fear.

I do know that some of my family and friends had an idea of what I was dealing with. They tried to talk to me about depression and anxiety. I brushed it off, declaring to myself and the world that this was just a phase—something I was "going through." I certainly wouldn't see a doctor for it. I wouldn't try to get to the root of it. I would just secretly search the internet for other people like me who couldn't drive, or go shopping, or sit in a crowded room.

I found those people. I discovered a few helpful articles that gave me insight into how I might get through this time of acute panic. While coping mechanisms are extremely helpful, they are only truly effective if used in conjunction with treatment. The component I was missing was a professional counselor to help me understand this vast world of anxiety that I had previously been a stranger to. Anxiety and depression are no small obstacles, and should be attacked with every arsenal possible. One's guard must be let down to deal with the underlying issues.

And in all of this, the driving motivation was control. I wanted to appear to be in control, even if that was the farthest thing from the truth. The truth was I had lost all control. I couldn't face the world and win and I knew it. And, at that point in my journey, I was content with lying to myself and those around me, if it meant I could postpone my reality as a person who suffered with anxiety and depression. I didn't want to be one of "them." I wanted to be the strong one; the woman who had more courage than most, who would fight with heroism and win at life. To me, admitting I was suffering from depression wasn't courageous. Admitting to a reality that included irrational fear wasn't brave. In my mind, I was strong when I suffered silently. Although I would nod with understanding when people would share their own struggles with anxiety, I kept my own experiences locked up inside. I lived in isolation and loneliness, peering through the blinds of my house, and my heart.

Journal Exercise

Are you hiding what is really going on in your life?

In what areas do you need to trust someone and share your pain?

_____

_____

_____

_____

_____

_____

_____

_____

_____

_____

_____

_____

"For God has not given us a spirit of fear, but of power and of love and of a sound mind."

2 Timothy 1:7 (NKJV)

2
The Assured Agoraphobic

We moved from Florida shortly after the birth of our first child. With everything I was feeling, it seemed like the worst possible idea. It would involve leaving everything I had known, to acclimate to a new city, home, and church. With all that I was facing in my emotional health, I wondered how I would manage the change of location. My husband, Brian, had accepted the invitation to serve as a Youth Pastor at a small, charming church in the beautiful state of Tennessee. There was no way I could have known how much this time in our life would contribute to the mending of my mind. It was here that I learned to take baby steps towards bravery. It was the loving people in our church who would unknowingly hold our hearts and our hands as we navigated a frightening journey.

Even the most timid of characters can at times put on a brave face, and enter into the drama of life with an assured demeanor. Some of us are even experts in the field of this kind of helpful hypocrisy. I excelled in this exercise. I was told once that I deserved an Oscar for my acting, because my friends had no idea I was struggling. My friends have informed me that during that time I came across assured, confident, and focused.

Those traits were the farthest thing from reality the evening we arrived in the charming town of Clinton, TN. My heart was pounding as we drove up to what would be our new apartment, to immediately spend time with our new parishioners. They were there to help us move in, and then spend the rest of the evening eating and begin getting to know each other a little.

I suppose it was a blessing that my allergies went into hyperactive mode, since they required me to ingest an antihistamine to help counteract my symptoms. My anxiety soon turned into medication induced apathy, as I struggled to stay awake. I sat, trying to have a conversation with the people we had arrived to minister to. I laugh now at the first impression I must have been making!

In the days and weeks that followed, I was able to settle into our new life with a certain level of success. I required help going to the grocery store, and making it to my appointments, but there was a reassuring peace that settled over me. Our little town was forgiving and kind. It seemed like the perfect location for healing. At that point I had no idea how long the road would stretch out before me.

I can remember nights when I would sit in bed, filling the pages of my journal with reflections about my state of mind, praying God would see fit to deliver me. I had days when I felt that I was making progress with my emotions, and other days when I would recoil in fear from the smallest of tasks.

Some of the hardest days were Sundays. I loved our church and the people in it, and yet there were weeks when I felt like I couldn't stand the thought of being surrounded by even a small crowd of churchgoers. They were so sweet, but I was equally scared. I was terrified of normal life; afraid to tell the truth about who I was. I was always stuffing my feelings down; pretending that the lump in my throat was only a figment of my imagination. I spent every church function hiding the truth about why I didn't want to participate, or doing my best to barely make it through.

One Sunday, I tried my best to enjoy the day with these people I loved so much, and yet I found myself once again hiding downstairs in the basement, crouched behind a closed door, begging God to deliver me. I was clever at finding a place to hide away from kind eyes who would find out the truth about my fear-filled days. I would cry in private and smile in public, hoping that I could get through a week without exposing my well-kept secret.

I was the assured agoraphobic. I crafted a demeanor that exuded courage and confidence, while living in fearful expectation something terrible was going to happen.

I never wanted to leave my home unless I was sure of the outcome. My heart pounded, and my breath came haltingly as I pulled out of the driveway and made my way into the sleepy community. Some days I could only handle one store, one appointment, one visit. Any more than that would leave me exhausted and on edge. I would feel dizzy and out of breath while doing the most routine tasks. I was always prepared for the worst, convinced if it could happen to anyone, it would happen to me. I was excruciatingly self-aware -- noticing every unusual sound, unfamiliar ache, and uninvited sensation that coursed through my surroundings, whether body or mind.

It was during this time that I cried out to God for deliverance.

And, I counted each trip to town without a panic attack as a certified victory. My heart would leap with excitement when I realized I was able to have lunch with a friend without escaping to catch my breath in the privacy of the bathroom. I could function in my fear. I could manage my misery. I *could* live. And yet, my small victories were short lived. My new reality was so different than anything I had ever experienced. I could hardly remember what it was like to go through the day without my heart pounding out of control.

I was somehow able to make it through the fog of fear and anxiety and enjoy being a mother to my little girl. Even during the hard days, one look at her sweet smile made me thankful to be alive. I suppose the desire to make her life better kept me going in the moments I didn't think I would make it.

Sometimes you just need to know that you can survive. Even though you may be struggling to wake up and live your version of normal, it has to be enough to just emerge each day a little more victorious than the last. I didn't know at that time that showing up was brave enough. That climbing up a mountain of uncertainty was courageous. I was so focused on the things I thought I couldn't do, that I missed noticing what God was giving me the strength to do.

Now I realize that a certain amount of mask wearing is normal, and even encouraged. We don't want to enter every single social function with all of our insecurities and messiness of life out there for everyone to see. We've all been around those people who spill every negative part of their life when you ask a simple "how are you?"

I would never advocate for that type of transparency. The kind where those around you are aware of every tragic detail in your life. There is a time and place for those kinds of conversations, but spilling all the bad parts of our lives on every unsuspecting individual that approaches us is not encouraged, or socially acceptable.

On the flip side, more often than not, we tend to pull all the negative parts of our lives inside, hiding them from the viewing public. Even our closest friends are not aware of the intensely personal battles we are fighting. That kind of mask wearing is not or ever should be encouraged.

At that point, I didn't feel comfortable saying the words … "I have agoraphobia." "I am struggling with panic disorder." "I can't go to the grocery store without hyperventilating." "I wake up many nights in a cold sweat, and have no idea why."

My desire for others to perceive me as a confident individual overwhelmed my desire to be free. I would rather pretend than let the walls come down and allow vulnerability to rule the day. And the cost of keeping silent was high. I was never completely myself. I would paint a smile when I should have let the tears flow. I would hide away in my home, when I should have been throwing the door open wide, and running to the beautiful place of transparency where I would find the support of my truest friends.

One evening while at a women's retreat that took all my courage to attend, I was discussing life with a good friend of mine. In the quiet of our hotel room, I summoned enough courage to tell her a little portion of my story. I let her see just a glimpse of the real me. That tiny bit of truth-telling was liberating. If only I would have continued down that road a little further. In telling only a part of the truth, I continued to feed the lie, because I wouldn't be completely honest. I was only sharing enough to garner sympathy, when I should have been pursuing transparency. Looking back, I see that my exhilaration at telling even a small part of the truth was short-lived. I found myself right back where I had started. Lying to others, and most tragically, lying to myself.

I was a masterful artist at living this agoraphobic life. I knew how to paint a vivid picture for the world to see that disguised the tones of grey hiding underneath. I was an artful deceiver in a clever disguise.

But the disguise wasn't working well. It's easy to fake people out for a few hours maybe, but that kind of hidden life is not sustainable over time. Each time I displayed vulnerability, my armor began to crack. Suddenly, being myself felt less like an option, and more like a necessity. All the while knowing if I let the fear creep out and show its ugly face, there would be no hiding again. "They'll know my secret, and will never view me as brave again," I told myself.

If you find yourself in a similar situation, I encourage you to rid yourself of the disguise. Run—don't walk—towards a place of vulnerability and openness with the people who know you best. Don't be afraid to tell them what you are feeling. Don't let the fear of misunderstanding keep you from living an authentic life. Break down and cry if you need to. Tell the person you are talking to that you need to walk outside for a minute and take a breath. Do what you need to. Your sanity is worth far more than someone's perception of you. It doesn't matter. They don't live your life. They don't endure the pain you experience daily. And in my experience, more often than not, the humans who surround you will step up to the plate, lending you the empathy you so desperately need. Because we all have unique stories that sound eerily the same.

The people we see each week are fighting their own battles. Or, they have fought similar battles, and won. The experiences that have shaped them, and the reactions they learned to cultivate can be life-changing for you!

Wouldn't you know that as soon as I began to share those hidden pieces, I discovered nobody actually cared that I struggled with agoraphobia. They literally didn't care. It was such a relief. They were sympathetic, and even sometimes expressed that they too had gone through a similar period of time. There was no judgement; no condemnation. There was only varying levels of understanding.

This realization brought freedom. There is power in the knowledge that each one of us has parts we keep hidden, and perfection is never actually underneath the disguise we so carefully maintain.

Journal Exercise

Why do you think we struggle with hiding our imperfections?
Are you tempted to hide what is really
going on in your life, and why?

_____

_____

_____

_____

_____

_____

_____

_____

_____

_____

_____

_____

"The Lord shall preserve you from all evil; He shall preserve your soul. The Lord shall preserve your going out and your coming in from this time forth, and even forevermore."

Psalm 121:7-8 (NKJV)

3

Driving Distressed

(And other moments of desperation)

I've always liked safety. I can't say that I've ever enjoyed the feeling that accompanies fear. I realize that some people get a kick out of scaring themselves silly, but I can't say I understand that desire. I can remember many a night tiptoeing quietly to my parents' room because a thunderstorm was threatening to destroy my very existence. I could be a bit on edge whenever faced with a situation that felt slightly out of control.

It wasn't so much that I was inflexible when it came to life plans, but maintaining control over the outcome of my day has typically been a top priority. I'm not a bungee jumping kind of girl. While I don't believe this inclination to control was to blame for my panic crisis, it certainly didn't help when my life felt like it was spiraling out of control.

As you may recall, my first major experience with mind-bending anxiety occurred while driving. Following that experience, I came to the irrational conclusion that driving wasn't safe. At any moment something could happen on the road that would render me useless, and I couldn't stomach the thought of getting back in the car. In someone living with panic and anxiety, a feeling of control can be vital to one's peace of mind. If there is even a slight chance that the day, the hour, or even the minute will end unpleasantly, it causes those with control issues to recoil at the thought. When someone experiences an anxiety attack, all rational thought escapes their mind, so situations that seem unmanageable pose a significant challenge.

There is a tendency for us with anxiety to overthink this issue. To fear people will assume labeling oneself a "control freak," is simply an excuse for fearful behavior. Perhaps indicative of a desire to gloss over issues in one's life that need to be rooted out and dealt with. The truth is that a lot of people struggle with control. Even if someone is not an overly selfish person, we all prefer achievable--desirable outcomes in life. There are a very few number of people who wake up each day hoping for the worst possible thing to happen to them.

For most of us, our desire for control stems from a desire to be IN control. We don't like the idea that someone out there might be responsible for what happens to us, and that despite our best efforts, we cannot ultimately change our course.

This is not to say that a change of course is not sometimes beneficial and necessary. However, even the most careful, healthiest, resourceful people encounter trying times. We all could tell stories of people who ate well all their lives, exercised daily, seemed the picture of health, and yet met an early death. Our minds reel at the idea, that in spite of our best efforts, the bleakness of life will take over, and we will be forced to accept our fate.

For me, the two hardest areas to admit I couldn't control were driving and flying. I had never struggled with either of those fears until my hormonal changes kicked into high gear. Suddenly, this unwelcome anxiety was taking over the pragmatic, logical section in my brain, and telling me that I was destined to meet a terrible fate in some kind of moving vehicle. I couldn't tell myself I would be okay. My mind had been hijacked and was lying to me on a regular basis.

When you are anxious, there is no common sense. People could list all the reasons why it was safe to be in a car or a plane, and my mind would scream back at them, "What if?! You don't know it will be okay!" My tendency toward negative thinking was compounded when I felt out of control. I couldn't relax. I couldn't live in the moment, because I was convinced that even my happiest moments were out to get me.

Truthfully, until one has felt the imagined clutches of death in moments that are ordinary, they cannot comprehend this phenomenon. There is no way to explain the lack of logic to someone who hasn't been there. And those of us who have faced this reality wish we could go back to simpler times and start over again. We want to overcome things that seem insurmountable, and become the people we dreamed of as children.

Take a moment to think back to when you were young. Most of us thought we were capable of doing anything. I can recall many a daydream that filled my mind, urging me to reach for the stars, or even the moon. Irrational fear doesn't typically begin for no reason.

We are born to thrive. We are fashioned to create. We want the best, and when encouraged we believe we can reach it.

"I can't" had never been a part of my vocabulary. I wanted to change the world from the time I knew the world needed help. I was blessed with great encouragement, from friends, family, and most notably, my parents. They were remarkable at lifting me up and preparing me for life's journey as a world changer. And most of the world changers I knew didn't let driving a car stop them in their tracks.

All the correct thinking, and encouraging words could not prepare me for the moment I came face to face with my own mortality. I wasn't ready for the time when my lack of coping skills met an ordinary situation, and turned it into a life-altering emergency.

Driving a car. Being responsible for another human being. Coming to grips with the fact that I couldn't control *anything*. All of it morphed into one big scary moment, and I was thrown into a sea of uncertainty, where the waves of despair drowned out my ability to whisper calming thoughts to my oxygen starved body. When you can't breathe, you can't think. And, when you can't think, you make decisions that are faulty at best.

There were underlying reasons for this panic that I wouldn't discover for many years. But, perhaps to a small degree my fear of driving was a living metaphor for another fear beneath the surface. Ultimately, I didn't like looking down the road of life with the realization that speed bumps were coming. There is something terrifying about cruising down a path without a clue as to what will happen. It brings a level of panic to those of us living with control-induced anxiety.

To this day there are times when I am stopped at a stoplight and feel this desire to drive as fast as I can away from the lane I am "stuck" in for the moment. Why? I don't like being told I need to stay in that spot. And I've discovered that I don't like being told by anyone (including God, if I'm honest) that I need to stay still for a moment. Waiting. Resting. Staying faithful in even a small moment. "No!" I scream in the quiet of my mind. "I want to move. I want to walk. I want to leave this place of waiting."

I've learned valuable lessons because of this fear. I remember hearing a still, small voice one day while waiting at a stoplight. I knew that God was helping me to learn that sometimes I'm asked to wait. Life isn't always about moving. There are times that require us to wait—be still—practice patience. Patience is a virtue which requires cultivating.

There is freedom that comes from the realization that the space I'm in at the moment is the one I'm supposed to occupy now. I may need to wait here and be faithful in this moment for reasons I can't see. Just as the stoplight is there to help the flow of traffic, so moments of rest and waiting can be for the good of those around us, as well as to keep us safe. When the light changes to green, we ease our way out into the flow of traffic once again. And when the time is right in our lives, we get moving in the direction that is best. For many of us, however, the waiting—the being still causes distress.

Depending on how one experiences distress there are usually physical reactions that occur during a moment of panic. One of two things typically happen. Either your emotions get so high until they inevitably spill out of your head, your eyes, and most unfortunately, your mouth. Or, you squash the emotions down, become very quiet, and run out of the room. Well, technically both of those scenarios might end with you running from the room; but, you can see how running is quite problematic when you find yourself locked in an airplane at 20,000 feet, or in the middle of a busy interstate, with no exit ramp in sight. Ugh.

I have never enjoyed the person I was (am) in those two scenarios, and my guess is my family and friends weren't particularly fond of me in that state either. They probably wondered why my eyes bugged out of my head when driving, or why I was annoyingly hypervigilant. Or, perhaps why I was huddled in the corner, moaning softly with my eyes shut (I kid; well, kind of). I probably muttered some inarticulate nonsense about the reason I was behaving that way in order to push aside any idea forming in their mind that I was a nutcase. Remember, I was not going to be "that" person. The one that needed a Xanax before boarding a plane.

As I look back at the most anxiety riddled portions of my life, I see something interesting. I didn't necessarily look down on people who struggled with anxiety. I didn't see depression as the unforgivable sin. I didn't think that someone dealing with mental illness was less of a person. And yet, I still subconsciously attached a stigma with those issues. I didn't want to be seen as a part of that group. The last thing I wanted was to be the focal point of someone's furtive glances and the topic of one's judgmental whispers.

What I've come to realize is that every single human being deals with weakness on some level. We don't have everything together. We can't be all we want to be every moment of the day. And that's perfectly okay. I believe banding together as a group of imperfect individuals who are sympathetic to each other's failings is much more enticing than living a lie and encouraging others to do the same.

We don't need someone to join us in our pity party and encourage us to settle into a life of adaptation. What those of us with mental illness need is someone who says, "I understand that you are going through something that seems never ending, but I'm here for you. We can be broken and scared together, but I will always encourage you to be the best 'you' there is."

No one wants to ignore problems, and live a second rate life. We want to hop in the driver's seat and ignore the scary voices in our head telling us we will fail. We want to rise up and be world changers, even on the days we can barely make it out of our beds. We want to make a difference in this life, and we need to be encouraged.

One of the ways I believe that anxiety ridden people need encouragement is in the form of empowerment. By empowerment, I mean that people who struggle with anxiety and depression are often high achievers—driven by wanting to make a better tomorrow. However, those same people are often bound by perfectionism and overwhelming feelings of inadequacy. Our flaws lie to us and tell us we aren't good enough to make a difference in a world that seems more perfect than us.

What I needed was for someone to look me in the eye, and tell me that I only had to keep taking one step at a time. If it meant that I would still run out of the room at times due to the fear that choked the life out of me, that was okay. There were times I felt like I should be stumbling through life in a better fashion. That somehow I had to live a more perfect existence … you know, the one with the picket fence, the gleaming kitchen, and the freshly-bathed children.

I believed the lie that I couldn't be a world-changer unless my ducks were in a row, my teeth were flossed, and my house was vacuumed. It took me several years to figure out that most of the people I knew who were making a difference did so while being a bit of a mess. They just got out there and "did." They didn't wait until the perfect time to jump. They chose to be fearless—to be brave—to be enough in the moment when it mattered.

In the times when I was terrified to drive, fly, or do anything that left me feeling powerless, I was forgetting that ultimately I wasn't in control anyway. I was putting myself in the driver's seat ... literally. In those moments I was not letting God be who I said I believed He was.

The truth is, my time is up when God says it is. I believe in being responsible and employing safety when choosing activities. However, when it comes down to it, the best place to be is living a purposeful life, and allowing God to decide the rest. The safest place to be is in the center of God's will. We have to leave the rest up to Him.

Now, when I drive my car down the interstate, I pray when I feel uneasy. I say something to the effect of "God, my time is in your hands. You are in control of my life, this car, and this road. Help me do what you've called me to do." Now, when I board the airplane, and feel those familiar pangs of anxiety when the flight attendant closes the door, I close my eyes, and say a similar prayer. "God, you are in control of my life, this airplane, the pilot, and the skies we are about to sail through. I am in your hands."

Well, that, and it doesn't hurt to have a Xanax tucked carefully away in my purse ... just in case.

Journal Exercise

What are the things in your life that you are trying to
control at the moment, even though you know deep
down you don't have power over the situation?

_____

_____

_____

_____

_____

_____

_____

_____

_____

_____

_____

_____

Journal Exercise

"*Worrying is carrying tomorrow's load with today's strength- carrying two days at once. It is moving into tomorrow ahead of time. Worrying doesn't empty tomorrow of its sorrow, it empties today of its strength.*"

— *Corrie ten Boom*

4

The Panicked Pastor's Wife

If you haven't grown up in the church world, you may not be aware of the expectations associated with Pastors' wives. It's a special kind of image. One that is a combination of Paula Dean and Jackie O - having just the right amount of stylist flair while putting on a killer Sunday lunch. Not only is there the assumed pressure to enter into each situation with a smile and sweet disposition; it doesn't hurt if you have class and culinary prowess. Throw in a side of playing the piano, and you have it made.

I was aware of these unspoken *restrictions* for the elite "Pastor's Wife Club" because I had grown up in a ministry family. In fact, when I found out the boy I had a crush on (who is now my husband) was pursuing a Ministerial degree, I secretly prayed he would reconsider. I wanted no part of the Pastor's Wife Club. I knew the pressure, and didn't want to participate.

How ironic that my husband would pursue ministry, and would end up on staff at a precious little Wesleyan Church in the hills of Tennessee. With trepidation, I embarked on the journey towards pastoral perfection. At least, that was my intention. Thankfully, all those piano lessons paid off, giving me one unspoken requirement under my belt. And, I could sing a little too, so I was able to fill a special music slot every so often. Well, I would have been able to more, if I wasn't so stinking scared all the time. My throat would tighten and tears would threaten to fall every time I neared the stage.

On top of all of this, I wanted to entertain, but how could I have a group of people to my house if the menu wasn't perfect and the rooms weren't spotless? If I was going to entertain, I was planning on beating Martha Stewart for top homemaker of the year. That seemed like one of the most important priorities to me during my first few years as a Minister's wife.

There is an assumption, whether real or imagined, that you have to be a certain kind of woman. That hospitality, mercy, service, and public speaking should come easily to you. While most people wouldn't say that out loud, there is a level of expectation from the church world as a whole. Some churches are more old-fashioned in this way, and place a high importance on the role of the wife, while others are realizing that it shouldn't matter what type of personality their leader's wife has. And while churches should be very careful how much pressure they place on the spouse of their leader, it is inevitable that some expectations will continue to exist.

Thankfully, both of the churches my husband and I have been part of have been very understanding and kind. If they did have expectations, they did well at hiding them. Over the years, people have embraced us, and allowed me the space to be who I am. That's not to say I haven't felt pressure. But, I wonder if at times it was due to my own personality as an overachiever. The desire to feel respected and valued in the role I've been called to has at times put unnecessary stress on me.

One of the first ways I wanted to appear as legitimate was in the way my family was dressed, and in how we conducted ourselves. It probably didn't help that our first church was in the South. It seemed there were unspoken rules of decorum that were beautiful and enduring. Once again, I think I was somewhat nearsighted in assuming I was required to be a certain kind of person and project a perfect persona. Looking back, I don't believe it was necessary, or required. Just because every southern kid said "Yes, Ma'am," and "Yes, Sir," when spoken to didn't mean I would be excommunicated if my child forgot to do that. It's easy to assume that people are monitoring you, when they really aren't.

I've done that all my life—worried what people thought of me. Part of that is because when you grow up in a ministry family, you are encapsulated in a fishbowl-type of life. There are people watching you all the time. Even if your parents shield you from the discussion, you know it's happening. You can see the looks in the faces of the people you serve. They are either beaming with pride, or examining you with smug curiosity.

It's pretty clear how this could present a problem to this panicked Pastor's wife. I was already dealing with my own agoraphobic tendencies, which basically meant that I didn't want to be on any kind of stage, where embarrassment was a possibility. Suddenly being thrust onto a different kind of stage—the one where your entire life is fair game, made me keenly aware of my impending humiliation.

It didn't matter if no one else saw it that way. A hundred people could tell me they weren't rooting for me demise. My perception was that everyone must be waiting for me to fail. I worried about what I said, how I looked, and whether or not I was adding any value to my husband's ministry.

People would often compliment my husband and I to our family members when they were visiting. They would talk of how much they loved our family and what we were doing. I remember feeling a small twinge of relief. To know that at least in some respects we were making a difference in someone's life, and yet, if I'm honest, I always wondered if they really meant it. How could they mean it, when they weren't aware of what a mess I was on the inside? At least that's what I wondered. Did they love us for who we were, or for the image we portrayed? I'll never know for sure, because at my first ministry experience I was less than honest about my true emotional state. Knowing the people we were surrounded with, I have no doubt I would have been loved, accepted and cared for in a meaningful way. The people we served were some of the best people I have ever been privileged to know. My choice to live in the shadows denied me the possibility of seeing what love in action may have looked like from that sweet little church.

My coming out as a panicked pastor's wife happened instead among the people of Nampa, Idaho. We moved there when our two oldest girls were three years and eighteen months. It was a leap of faith, as we were going to a part time position that paid barely enough to make a rent payment. The irony of this position was huge, because it was the one place we said we would never go.

My husband was raised in the area, and we were going to be on staff at the church where he grew up. We were literally going to be pastoring family members at this church. Talk about pressure! Even Christ addressed the issue of prophets not having honor in their own country (Mark 6:4). What were we thinking?

Even if we weren't thinking, God had a plan bigger than we could have ever imagined. We moved with cautious optimism. We moved in with my in-laws for the first few months, and started the process of exploring a new town and enjoying new possibilities.

I remember the first Sunday in great detail. There were familiar faces, because this was the place Brian came "home" to on holidays. I remember entering the foyer of the church, walking with an air of counterfeit confidence and a new haircut. I was going to rock this pastoral gig. I was going to shake every church-goer's hand, and smile my way through the nervousness I pushed below the surface of my butterfly companions.

I believe it was one of the very first Sundays that someone approached me about joining the worship team. They had heard that I could play the piano and sing, and felt I could be a blessing to their group. I recall laughing and shrugging it off, all the while knowing that I would need to engage in some type of ministry in the near future. I wasn't ready to be pushed past the limits of my comfort zone at that point, but I had this strange suspicion that I wasn't going to have a choice.

There was no way we could have known the ways that we would be stretched. I set my course to figure out who I was supposed to be in this new sea of faces. I admit I was a little wobbly at first. In fact, it took me a few years to get my sea legs. I wasn't in love with my new city, and wasn't sure what my role was in this season of life.

Most of the time, I just tried to be the best Mommy I could to my two little girls. Once we settled into our small rental house, I spent my days arranging it to suit my taste, and figuring out one hundred ways to stretch a dollar.

I look back at those days with fondness—our little family of four against the world. We were learning new ways to do things. We were stretching our wings, taking off, and flying most of the time. My husband was busy working two jobs to make ends meet, and I was making sure I did everything I could to project the image of appropriateness to the churchgoers, some of them being extended family.

I did join the worship team, and started playing the piano every once in a while. And every time I did, the same thing would happen. Fear would grip my chest so tightly that I wondered if I would leave the stage alive. I pushed myself to continue, because I was determined to use the gifts I had been given by God. I was under the impression that good pastor's wives did what they were supposed to. Their gifts were given to glorify God. I believed my life was supposed to be entrenched in ministry no matter how I felt. I was determined to project an air of confidence and capability, even if I knew the truth—that I was hopelessly underqualified. I had gifts to offer, but I wasn't in a place emotionally to give what was being asked of me. I wish I had told myself to take some time to adjust and quit trying to live up to a perceived expectation.

If there is one thing I could tell others who find themselves at the start of a new job, position, or anything that requires an adjustment period, it would be to chill out and let life calm down before jumping into any version of people pleasing. On that note, maybe we should all just walk away from any objective of trying to be something we're not. It's exhausting.

The way I look at it (now, after approximately ump-teen years of pandering), there is no plausible reason to project an image of anyone other than ourselves. It's not so much that we say "This is me ... so deal with it." I much prefer the version of myself that works hard to grow in the areas that I am lacking. However, when we accept the fact that we are fearfully and wonderfully made by a Creator who has a greater purpose in mind, amazing things can happen.

I can tell you that the worrying I participated in during my early years as a ministry wife did nothing for my pastoral progress. It didn't create a stronger me. In fact, I believe it held me down. I was so stressed half the time, that I became a monster when it didn't count, and an illusion when I thought someone was watching. That meant that while everyone at church and at social functions thought I was a strong, spiritual woman, my family knew the opposite. That I was an emotionally fragile person, who was crying inside while pretending I was the brave one in the room.

The church world got the "put-together" me, and my family was on the receiving end of the "panic-stricken" me. The one who snapped when life was stressful. The one who lied all the time about who she was. The one who caved when chaos came calling. And, I regret to tell you that all the beautiful storybook moments we shared couldn't make up for the nightmares I experienced behind closed doors. I would collapse in a heap after coming home from yet another ministry opportunity and wonder if it would ever get easier.

The drama that unfolded over the next few years was a far cry from anything I would have wished to look back on as the story of my life. But, it has served a monumental purpose in my life. It has taught me lessons that I never wish to repeat, but that I am willing to share with the rest of the class.

Lesson number one: Be you. Don't try to live in someone else's shoes. Don't run a race that you haven't paid the entrance fee for. It's exhausting, and trust me, you aren't ready for it. I'll admit I still struggle with this one. I would rather be the girl I think has life figured out—the one who doesn't seem to be afraid of anything. There are times I've wished for a different personality. But, I have to surrender that tendency. And you should to! Allow the world to enjoy the uniqueness of who God created you to be. Find out what your qualities and gifts are. There are so many resources out there to help guide you on the path to understanding how you are wired. Use them. Discover who you are, and then rest. Rest in the personhood that you have been blessed with. You have boundless potential!

Lesson number two: Quiet yourself before God and let Him guide you. So much of human existence is spent striving, and I believe we've lost the art of stillness. Rest in God's provision and grace. Inhale the beautiful air that He gives you and exhale the doubt, worry and fear. Trying to keep up with an elusive version of yourself is wearing you out. You are loved, no matter what you accomplish, so quit making it about how good you are. Christ has already done the work for you. Accept His free gift.

Lesson number three: While you give yourself room to be who you are, give yourself the gift of purposeful inspection. Examine your life. What should you be spending your time improving? If you find yourself in a rut, work at getting out. Acceptance of who you are is no excuse for laziness. Don't wallow in self-pity. Work at your shortcomings not from the need to impress, but rather from the desire to improve. There is a definite difference between the two extremes.

Finding a balance in these areas is difficult at best, but I can assure you, it's possible. When you find yourself striving ... stop. When you find yourself reaching ... rest. When you see a bent to perfectionism ... pause. Ask God to show you the deepest layer of your need to impress, and ask Him to remove the inclination to serve that desire.

You were created on purpose. You matter, just the way you are. Stop pretending to be the perfect version of the person you think you should be. Figure out how to be the best version of you, and let that be enough.

Journal Exercise

Do you feel the pressure to perform? In which areas do you want to find freedom from the need to impress? Which areas do you know you need to grow in—to make strides to be better?

_____

_____

_____

_____

_____

_____

_____

_____

_____

_____

_____

_____

"In the multitude of my anxieties within me, Your comforts delight my soul."

Psalm 94:19 (NKJV)

5
Nursery Nightmares

I've been told I'm bossy, although in my early years I would heartily disagree with anyone who would label me as such. I have always known that God gifted me with the ability to coordinate people effectively in order to get a job done with excellence (that sounds better than bossy). However, in the past I have cringed at the added responsibility required to manage a group of people. And, of course there's the added potential of losing control when working with other humans.

I'm a bit of a fixer. I like nothing better than to solve a problem I see right in front of me. I like to fill needs when they present themselves. During the early years at the church in Nampa, I especially enjoyed doing jobs that were done behind the scenes. I could clean toilets like a boss, and I preferred serving in that kind of ministry.

Imagine my surprise when I heard myself saying yes to the

question of whether or not I would take over the position of Nursery Coordinator. I felt peace, but it certainly was going to be out of my comfort zone. This kind of position was a leap for the "anxious" me, because I would have a great degree of responsibility. Still, I agreed to it, because in my mind, it couldn't be that hard to coordinate childcare for one service a Sunday.

It turned out to be harder than I thought it would. Anyone who has directed a nursery ministry will attest to the stress involved with caring for the littlest church members. I entrenched myself in the process; pouring over schedules, making calls to nursery workers, and organizing the rooms in new ways in order to make the Sunday morning experience better. I was determined to be the best Nursery Coordinator any church had ever seen.

Part of my role required that I work alongside two other children's ministry leaders. At that point in my life, I was a mess when it came to any kind of crucial conversation. I hadn't thought through all the ways I would be stretched when I said yes to the position. I remember one meeting in particular that required a difficult decision. As we were discussing and brainstorming, my heart was racing. I felt as if I had to stuff it back down my throat. I willed myself to stay in my seat and have this conversation. I was completely undone on the inside, but was doing everything within my power to keep the appearance of having it together. I couldn't think of the important things I needed to say. I couldn't make my words come out right, and I wanted to break down and cry.

I found myself having this reaction to meetings in general. When decisions had to be made, when discussions had to be held, I buckled under the pressure of it. I cowered in the presence of conflict, even when it was of the healthy variety. I preferred to work in isolation, carefully planning all details on my own—placing all the responsibility for success and failure on my own shoulders.

That was obviously not an acceptable or effective way to operate a children's program, so I had to become capable of discussing ideas, plans, and assignments without worrying I would end up with a giant panic attack.

Kids seem to manage life much better when their leaders show confidence under pressure. They want to know that the person in charge of them is stable and capable of meeting their needs. Because this prerequisite for running children's ministry existed, I learned to fake it till I could make it.

Sunday mornings were often a blur. Arriving early, I would make sure everything was in its proper place. You could find me, at the crack of dawn, unloading a dishwasher, and carrying a large bowl of sippy cups to the nursery. I would wave and smile at people as I walked by, armed with an imagined confidence in my ministry position. Now mind you, I had three small children, with one on the way during this time. I not only had to make sure my ministry was operating effectively, but I also had to function as a Mom.

Some mornings I would arrive at the church, begin my preparations, and my phone would buzz with two or three text messages of people who were canceling at the last moment. "Breathe." I remember telling myself to calm down. "I can handle this," I would recite to myself over and over. And I would. Through God's grace, and some fantastic deep breathing skills, I would typically avoid the panic stage of anxiety. And then there were the days when I was ducking in and out of the rooms, trying not to bring attention to the fact that I could barely stand up straight due to dizzying anxiety.

But, I refused to let it take me out. I was determined to keep moving, one step at a time.

God used that time in my life to teach me some important lessons that have served me well in my growth as a leader. This experience provided invaluable stepping stones which I was able to walk with confidence in other areas of my life

First, I learned how to organize my time effectively. I couldn't wing it. I needed to focus in order to facilitate the systems that the church and I had put into place. As a creative personality, I was accustomed to living minute to minute. While flexibility is a good quality, it's important to focus on creating order and stability when leading a team. As the leader of a department, it was imperative that I learn the art of "prioritization." For those of us who don't particularly like being put in a box, these lessons are extremely valuable.

Second, I acquired the important skill of managing a team. I was in charge of at least six people every Sunday, which meant dealing with almost thirty individuals throughout the span of a month. Different personalities, ministry ideas, and philosophies collided into one team. I also dealt with the different obstacles present within the ages of children, newborn to five. It was the perfect amount of healthy stress for me to experience growth. I wouldn't have been able to handle the responsibilities I took on with later ministries without this valuable time of instruction.

Lastly, I learned to give God my problems. The phrase "Let go. Let God" always seems flippant and unrealistic to me. I've always been a fixer. I can typically make things happen, even if I'm not relying on Someone outside of myself. This time, I found myself in situations I couldn't figure out, and in problems I couldn't solve on my own. I *had* to rely on God. To this day, when I encounter a ministry challenge, I remember the moments I thought were impossible and how God showed up. I pray differently because of the specific answers to prayer I was blessed to witness during that season. God used this period of my life to teach me about blind faith. He taught me to trust that He was good enough to handle my problems … no matter how insignificant they might seem.

There were many times when I would be overwhelmed by the process of faith. I remember moments in which my fear and anxiety would threaten to take over as I worked on schedules, aware there weren't enough people to fill the slots needed. God's provision was evident every single week. During the days when I was about to lose it, He was there, inviting me to let Him in on my problem and allow Him to provide the solution He was there, steadily, and faithfully teaching me to lean into Him. To call on Him when life got tough—to trust Him.

I can tell you from experience that willingness to serve, even in obscure areas will pay off in life-changing ways. The opportunity to learn life lessons is often found in seemingly unimportant positions.

It can be tempting to discount what we might do behind the scenes. But, the learning you do in the background can be life changing when the work you do suddenly moves to the foreground. The diligence in everything you do behind the scenes pays off later; so work with excellence. Even in those moments which seem difficult when you are tempted to shrug it off because, "after all, you just work in the background." Don't limit what God can teach you through these seemingly insignificant moments.

Those moments were what launched me into believing that I could be stretched beyond what I had previously thought. God's hand of protection, provision, and promise was there, lifting me up when I walked a seemingly impossible path. Walking on those impossible paths taught me life-changing lessons in perseverance.

Let me tell you a little about what perseverance can mean in a life filled with anxiety or depression. Perhaps you find yourself in a such a season right now. You feel like you can't keep moving. You are afraid of failing. And, you certainly aren't growing.

Can I let you in on a little secret? The road to success is paved one step at a time. You have to dig in and keep moving. Even on the days you don't feel like it. Dig in. Don't let fear control you. Don't let it have the upper hand. Look it square in the face and declare with your entire being, "You won't win."

Even when it seems like things aren't going right. Even on days that you can hardly get out of bed. Just do the *next thing*. Wake up. Rise up. Move forward. Imagine the day when you will kick fear out completely. But, until that day comes, reach for the courage inside of you that comes during your moments of intense fear. When you think you can't keep moving … move anyway. When you don't know which step to take … take one anyway. When everything is caving in on you, push away the debris with your weakened arms, and cry, "You won't win … I'm not going to let you win."

The secret to living a life of courage in the midst of anxiety is relatively simple. *Just do it*. You may have wished for a better formula, or a step by step process. But, let me assure you, from my experience, the most important thing you can do is to *just move*. Remember it's not brave if you're not scared.

If you can get up each morning, get dressed, brush your teeth and eat breakfast … you've won a little.

If you can make your bed, do the dishes, and do something to develop yourself … you've won a little more.

If you can walk outside, get in the car, and drive down the road ... you are on your way to a life of uncommon courage.

As one who has lived every single day with the cloud of anxiety over my head, let me tell you, there is hope. There is always hope.

Persevere.

Don't give up.

Get out of bed, brush those teeth, and start the day.

You can do this.

Journal Exercise

Is there an area in your life where you
need to "just do the next thing?"
In what areas do you need to persevere?

_____

_____

_____

_____

_____

_____

_____

_____

_____

_____

_____

Say to those with fearful hearts, "Be strong, and do not fear, for your God is coming to destroy Your enemies. He is coming to save you."

Isaiah 35:4(NLT)

6

Medicine, Marriage & Milestones

*Note: Please understand that what I am sharing with you in this chapter is my personal journey. Medication is very useful and necessary for many people. Always consult your Doctor and/or Licensed Counselor for advice concerning treatment.

For four years I existed with the agonizing reality of unwelcomed adrenaline surges. It didn't rule every minute of my day in the beginning, but over the course of those four years it increased to the extent that I couldn't function. My life was defined from one panic attack to another. I think I must have believed that one day all of this mental anguish would magically disappear. I refused to seek counseling for many years and I certainly wouldn't consider medication as the right choice for me.

I was naive enough to believe that my body could handle the overwhelming stress it was dealing with on a regular basis. My version of living life wasn't life at all. During the worst season of my struggle with anxiety I barely made it a day without some kind of attack. I dreaded sleep, because my mind would race and my body would be jolted awake by some unknown fear-inducing emotion. I was acutely aware that I was not in control of my body or my mind.

At this point, even avoidance couldn't rescue me from my irrational fears. Moments of normalcy became scarce and I wondered if I would ever find myself again.

One day, while braving a Bible study, I received a comforting promise from God. It was the moment I look back on as my turning point. As we turned to the passage we would be studying that day, my eyes fell on a verse that wasn't even part of our lesson! It seemed as if it leapt off the page.

> *Say to those with fearful hearts, "Be strong, and do not fear, for your God is coming to destroy your enemies. He is coming to save you."*

> *Isaiah 35:4 NLT*

Tears burned at the back of my eyes, begging to escape. I knew that God was getting my attention. Just that week I had been questioning whether or not He really cared about the many times I had begged Him to rescue me from the enemy of anxiety. And there it was …

> *Say to those with fearful hearts, "Be strong. Do not fear. Your God is coming to destroy your enemies. He is coming to save you."*

If I'm confident of anything, I'm confident He was giving me a promise. And as the days turned into weeks, and the weeks turned into months, it became clear that the promise was being fulfilled.

Not long after that encounter in Isaiah, I found myself at rock bottom physically. It had become so difficult that my body wouldn't even work correctly. I remember a couple of days in which I could do nothing except lie very still on the couch. Every part of my body hurt. And yet, I knew I wasn't just physically sick. I had some understanding that there was something wrong with me on a cellular level.

I finally made an appointment with my Doctor and had Brian drive me to it. As I finally let everything spill out to someone who had the power to help me, the tears began to fall. I didn't want to say the words that were coming out of my mouth. No one was supposed to find out I was weak. That I couldn't get through a day without a panic attack. That I couldn't sleep well. That my entire body ached with pain that was different from anything I had ever known. That I was fighting one of the biggest enemies I'd ever encountered.

I'll never forget the compassion on that man's face. He listened, and then he gently spoke the words that would change so much. "Your body is tired. Your body is sick." He explained that the years of living panic attack to panic attack had finally caught up with me. He helped me to understand that our bodies are not designed to take that kind of beating without relief. My mind was finally doing the right thing by telling me it was time to get help.

I didn't want to hear what he said next. I wanted to run out of that room and never come back again. I knew what was next. It was time to get some pharmacological help. He prescribed medication that was supposed to begin calming those places in my brain that wouldn't settle down. Let me tell you, it was everything I could do to make myself take that first pill. I was terrified. This was not the kind of weapon I had expected to use against this adversary. I wanted a miracle that didn't require me to take a man-made solution. I had heard the horror stories about medication. I was imagining every negative side effect as if it was a sure thing. I didn't know what would happen next, and I was frightened of feeling out of control.

I couldn't believe what happened after the first week of being on the medicine. My mind began to calm. I could see things around me that I hadn't seen for months. I noticed the funniest things— like how the grass smelled. Funny, I know, but my panic induced mind had filtered some of those simple things out just to survive. My mind was no longer overwhelmed by the speed at which it had been racing. I did have some adjustments to the medication that were difficult. One night the paramedics even had to be called as my body adjusted to the effects of the medication. This period of time was both calming and frightening. But, I felt peace that God was using this medication to save my life—He was saving me from the enemy of anxiety.

As I settled into my new normal, I was overjoyed at the way my life was getting back on track. I could sit in a crowded room without feeling out of my mind. I could go to church and enjoy it without the overwhelming desire to run away. I could drive to the store and handle a long line without hyperventilating. I could sleep, soundly, without a care in the world.

I did not achieve perfection with this new treatment, in fact there were some significant setbacks that I experienced. However, the Jamie before medication and the Jamie after it were remarkably different. And the change was good.

In the six years that I took that little pill, my life took a needed turn. I can't imagine what would have happened without the help of medicine. However, I wouldn't be honest if I didn't share the negative effects that became a part of my daily existence. With the welcomed changes came ones that I wished would go away. I became a different person in less welcomed ways. I gained forty pounds. I was sleepy when I didn't want to be. There were times I felt numb and wished for the ability to cry my eyes out again. Some of these effects were a part of the package. I didn't want to say goodbye to the good outcomes that were now a part of my life because of the medication. And yet, I was frustrated I had to deal with the side effects.

Looking back I can see some of the positive and negative parts of my journey. For instance, anxiety and depression, and the treatment for it can have significant effects on your marriage and family relationships. Anxiety turns you into an unrecognizable person, and depression can make you uninterested in those around you. Add in the numbing effects of medication, and you have a recipe for a unique challenge.

For years I lived through a cycle of emotions which I felt powerless to control. The treatment plan I was on helped so much in the day to day existence that was so important. Performing tasks like feeding and caring for my children, running simple errands, and handling a group of people became a possibility again. However, I now had to deal with a completely different kind of feelings indicator. I didn't cry like I use to. I didn't feel things like I use to—even feelings of love.

My medication helped take the edge off of my anxiety, but I was also dealing with some depression symptoms some of the time too. For a few years I wondered if I still loved my husband. I was numb and couldn't will myself to change. I tell you this because you may feel like you are the only one that has gone through this phenomenon. I remember wishing I could go back to being the person I was before, because at least I felt something.

After ten years of mental health challenges and necessary treatment, I hardly knew who I was anymore. There is no cut and dry answer to any of this. I couldn't figure out who the real Jamie was. I couldn't trust my feelings, because they were not longer a true indicator of what was going on in my mind.

Enter counseling.

Honestly, if I hadn't finally decided to put my fears aside and get help from a licensed Counselor, I don't know where I would be today. I can't stress this enough. Get help. Do it now.

It took me ten years to give in, but once I walked into that room, sat down and began sharing my story, everything changed. God placed me with incredible Counselors for a significant period of time, and the transformation has been remarkable. When I finally decided to begin that part of my healing journey, I dove in with everything I had. I went every week, cringing every time I paid the fee. I was determined to make it work if it killed me. I was going to get well, even if it meant figuring out a way to stretch the budget. I give an enormous amount of credit to my husband, Brian for this as well. He didn't always understand the process, but he allowed me to do what was needed.

Most days I left the counseling center in tears, with a pounding headache. I was going through a ridiculous amount of pain in order to tear down old thinking patterns and rebuild new ones. I was reliving old traumas and fears that I would have rather forgotten.

I was throwing myself into the fire in order to be made new. There were times when it seemed like the process to get well was more difficult than just staying where I was. As my treatment went on, I realized the days following my session were often the hardest. I would wake up with nightmares and cold sweats. I feared I would never be well. I really wondered if God was going to allow me to be healed.

One of the kindest ways that God showed His great love to me during this time was by what song would be playing on the radio when I would get in my car. Inevitably, the message would correspond with the issue I was dealing with. One day, I was wrestling with how long the process was taking. I wanted healing, and I wanted it right there in that moment. I had prayed and begged God to deliver me from my fears for the past ten years, and even while I was trying to get help, it seemed like my healing would never be realized. As I turned out of the driveway from the counseling center, the words and melody of this song filled my car.

I know the sorrow, and I know the hurt
Would all go away if You'd just say the word
But even if You don't
My hope is You alone
You've been faithful, You've been good
All of my days
Jesus, I will cling to You
Come what may

I'm pretty sure I cried the whole way home. I hit the steering wheel over and over, releasing pent up frustration. I was so done with this stupid problem. That's how I felt. I was stupid and this fear was stupid.

I wanted to believe the words of that song. I wanted to say I could cling to Jesus and be okay if God didn't make the sorrow and hurt go away with one word. I did a great deal of surrendering on the car ride home that day. And, I kept giving my grief and anguish to God every week as I went back for my sessions.

One of the best things to happen to me during this time was that I came to accept the fact that God loved me. I had lived so much of my life trying to be better so that I could earn God's affection. I needed Him to love me so that I was worthy to stand before Him. I had been dealing with a severe mental block regarding the idea that God loved me no matter what I did. If I didn't do one more good deed in my life, His love for me would not diminish. I couldn't grasp that concept.

The day I came face to face with the truth about how much God loved me is a day I'll never forget. The words "He loves you, He loves you, He loves you," played over and over in my mind.

Many years of incorrect thinking had led me to think of God as a bully who would give up on me any time I made a wrong move. I would be moved to tears by the verses found in Romans 8 which read, "For I am persuaded that neither death nor life, nor angels nor principalities nor powers, nor things present nor things to come, nor height nor depth, nor any other created thing, shall be able to separate us from the love of God which is in Christ Jesus our Lord." (v. 38-39 NKJV). I was moved, but it didn't penetrate my fearful heart.

One evening while tucking my children into bed, I paused by the side of one of my daughters. She was already sleeping, and I took a moment to gaze on her peaceful face. As I did, tears sprung into my eyes as I thought about how much I loved her. I thought about how I would never do anything to knowingly hurt her. I couldn't imagine if I allowed anything bad to happen to her.

I was broken in that moment because I became angry at God. I actually looked up at the ceiling with angry, tear filled eyes and demanded an answer. "How could you do this to me?" I asked. "I've done everything right. I was the good girl. I did nothing to deserve this!" I knew He could have kept me from this pain, and He didn't. He let it happen. And I was mad about it. I was crushed that I wasn't rescued from the uncontrollable spiral into the frightening world I now lived in.

This encounter was crucial to my healing. Because as I lashed out in frustration and anger, all I felt was compassion and love. I knew in that very moment He loved me enough to allow me to go through this journey. As a loving parent, I can't protect my children from every experience in life. In fact, some of the most frustrating moments to them are ones I know they need to go through for their good.

I began a journey of understanding that my life doesn't have to look perfect in order to be purposeful. I began to learn that His plans for me are good even when my days aren't that good. I can have a beautiful life of meaning even if the nights are long and my faith is tested.

As I began to experience breakthrough after breakthrough, my life began to change. My marriage began to change. My health began to change. I was able to handle moments of crisis with calm. My children didn't drive me as crazy as they had before. I began to live by faith in the moments when I was tempted to crumble. I felt like I was a walking miracle!

Now, to be sure, I had to do some significant work during this process. Take my marriage for instance. During the years that I felt numb and wondered if I even loved my husband anymore, I had a choice to make. I could have walked away from the marriage when things got tough. Worldly wisdom would say if you don't feel love, it's time to leave. I chose instead to pray daily for a miracle in that area of my life. When I was tempted to walk away and pretend my vows didn't matter, I pressed into my Savior and begged Him for His help. I chose love, when I didn't feel love. I remember days when I would pray and ask God to bring back the feelings like I had when I first met my husband. It seemed silly sometimes, praying those prayers. And yet, I believed that if I continued to be faithful, that God would meet me in that place of sacrifice. He did meet me where I needed Him most. My battle was taking everything out of me and I was holding on to a promise-keeping God. I began to feel strengthened in the areas that mattered most.

The day came, after years of praying the same prayer, that my butterflies came back. You know the ones you remember from your first few dates. That feeling of infatuation that you think is love, only to discover that it fades with time. Brian walked into the kitchen, and my heart skipped a beat. I looked into his eyes and felt like an emotional high schooler again. And I cried. Not an all-out sob fest—just a few tears of joy and thankfulness. The hard work and determination had paid off. The prayers I had prayed had been answered. My choice to love my husband when the feelings were gone had been rewarded.

I knew in that moment that our marriage would never be perfect, but that didn't matter—it still doesn't. All that matters is that we have weathered the storm, and we will keep weathering the storm … until death parts our ways.

If you are the spouse or loved one of a person going through a mental health crisis, can I just encourage you to keep going? The path won't be smooth. The days will be long, and the nights will be confusing. But, they. need. you. They need a loving heart and a steady hand. They need to hear that they are loved, no matter what. You will get tired and worn. You won't always understand the experiences they go through, but it will affect you both. Give them some space to work it out. Encourage them on their journey. If you're married, be faithful. I can promise you, it's worth it.

After going through counseling for seven months, I began the process of weaning off of my medication. I was under the supervision of my Doctor and Counselor to make sure I was okay during this process.

It was hard. After being medicated for six years, my body craved that serotonin. I remember waking up, dizzy, sweating, trying to calm myself down. Thankfully, I had coping mechanisms as a result of therapy, and I was able to make it.

I tried to watch what I ate, making sure I was getting protein, good carbohydrates, vegetables and fruit. I took vitamins and exercised at least three times a week. I was trying to assist my body during the time of weaning off.

It took about three and a half months to completely wean off the medication. I felt free and alive. I was able to walk through a normal day without anxiety and I finally felt like "me" again. I could cry again. I could feel emotions I hadn't felt in a long time. It was incredible.

You can imagine that after a decade of bondage, I was feeling pretty incredible. The fact that I had gone through so many ups and downs and was finally back to a version of normal absolutely astounded me. I experienced about five glorious months of freedom. I even told everyone around me how much God had done for me. I felt like a walking miracle.

And then, something happened that knocked me over. It was an ordinary day, and I was doing ordinary things. There was no reason for something to go wrong. There was no apparent trigger and I wasn't afforded the consideration of a warning.

The anxiety attack started slowly, as they often do. I felt the twinge in my chest and the dizzy feeling in my head. My breath started to come in gasps. I swallowed. I breathed slowly. I walked around the room, trying to get a grip on what was happening.

I walked down to my neighbor's house and told her I wasn't feeling well. I asked her to pray with me, which she did. I drank water - I ate a few crackers - We checked my blood pressure. Nothing was stopping the immovable force of a panic attack. Suddenly it was in full force, and I was on my way to the Emergency Room. I cried in between my gasps for air. I was confused and broken.

After tests were concluded, it was determined that it was only anxiety. Of course it was. I should have known that before the first poke.

"I'm still a mess," I told myself. "I'm a mess and I'm a fool."

I couldn't believe that after five months of freedom, I was experiencing the old me again. I didn't even know how to react. What had caused me to have such a sudden turn for the worse, I wondered?

I second guessed coming off my medication. I thought for sure the Doctor was going to insist I go back on it. He didn't. He suggested instead that I see my Counselor and make that a regular habit again before jumping to conclusions about the state of my mind.

I did see my Counselor and discovered that I had some significant things to work through. There were some unresolved memories that were coming to the surface (more on that in another chapter). I was also able to learn an important lesson. For many of us with anxiety or depression, challenging cycles will be a part of life. It doesn't mean we are broken … it means we are human. We might have weeks of normalcy and then suddenly something will happen that causes us to reach into our toolbox of coping skills and use them! And that's okay!

We have to get to the place where we are okay with necessary treatment. So many of us want to be strong on our own. We don't want to get the help we need, whether it be through people, or medicine. There is absolutely nothing shameful about taking what your body needs. We wouldn't tell a diabetic to go off of their insulin. We wouldn't deprive a cancer patient of their chemo. We wouldn't ask a person with a heart defect to give up their heart medication. Why should we treat deficiencies in the mind any differently? We might need treatment. We shouldn't feel like less of a person because we need to avail ourselves of life-giving therapies.

God equipped people to discover methods that can help the human race through all kinds of illnesses. Sometimes the way He heals is through the wisdom of another human. However, if you talk to anyone who has gone through any type of ailment, you will discover that the treatment was hard. The days were difficult. It typically doesn't involve a quick fix.

If there is one message I would wish to get across, it's that we have to ride the wave. When you look at the ocean and see those mighty, turbulent waves they look beautiful. But they are often messy and unpredictable, just like life. And yet, you see people riding them with apparent ease. Even the most experienced surfers get knocked off the wave, and have to make the choice to get back up and ride again.

We have to do that in our lives. Rough days will happen. Marriages will be strained from time to time. Raising kids will prove to try your patience. Bills will be more than your bank account. Difficult diagnoses will be discovered. Life will toss you about like a mighty wave, and there is only one way to make it work. Ride the wave. Get back on it and know that every time you do you are getting stronger.

Every next step is a milestone. Each little victory will turn into something greater as you keep moving. Life doesn't have to be perfect for you to make a difference. Start with your family. Start with your close relationships. Make the choice that you are going to ride the waves of difficulty and when you fall, get back up.

Choose surrender.

In the moments when you are tempted to doubt God's great love for you, look back at how He's carried you. I know it's not always easy in the moments when you are worn out from life. But, He has a plan for you and it's for your good. Trust Him in the details of your journey. He's got you.

Journal Exercise

In what areas do you know it's time to surrender?
Are there places in your life in which you
have allowed emotions to rule?

_____

_____

_____

_____

_____

_____

_____

_____

_____

_____

_____

_____

"I had the chance to make every possible mistake and figure out a way to recover from it. Once you realize there is life after mistakes, you gain a self-confidence that never goes away."

— Bob Schieffer

7
The Scary Stage

I am a musician who has grown up on a stage. From a very young age I've walked up stairs which led to a place of performance. Some has been for fun, but typically it's been for some kind of ministry.

While singing or performing in front of people had never been my favorite activity, I was able to do what was asked of me with relative ease. Once I began to experience anxiety, I avoided public speaking and anything similar like the plague. In fact, I dealt with unbelievable performance anxiety for over a decade of my life. Anytime I entered the stage, my heart would race, my breath came in gasps, and I would have to force myself to fill my lungs with the oxygen they desperately craved. The room would close in, the faces would become a blur, and my world would spin as I struggled against the terrifying grip of terror. If you've never experienced stage fright, *true* stage fright, I envy you. It has had a death grip on me too many times, and until recently, I found it difficult to walk across a platform and share my talents.

It hasn't been for a lack of trying. Like I said, I've grown up on the stage. From that precious Christmas pageant around the age of three, to the many evenings spent sharing with churches across the United States as a missionary family, I should be an expert in taming the nervous feelings that creep up inside my throat. As I think back over my life, it's almost comical. How can someone who has had incredible experiences and lived big portions of her life on the stage still have a problem with it? It's never made sense to me!

I've almost done it all: Plays, recitals, missionary services, state competition, choir, public relations group, playing piano for church, speech class, and leading worship. After all of these worthy endeavors, you'd think I could embrace the stage with gusto and excitement.

And yet, the struggle remained. It would be some time before I would come to realize one of the emotional triggers that was causing this paralyzing fear. I knew it was ridiculous. I told myself I needed to get over it. And, yet, there I was. Stuck between sharing my gifts, and shrinking in fear.

Some days were better than others. Varying levels of confidence would come and go, depending on factors I could never completely figure out. But, at the end of the day (or the recital), I left with a depleted reserve of serotonin, and an intense need for comfort food. I felt worn, frazzled, undone.

I had some people tell me that perhaps I should just realize my limitations, and stay away from an experience that would prove to be so taxing on my emotions. I can't say I disagreed with them. In fact, I remember feeling relief for a little while. I even walked away for a season. Why did I need to keep torturing myself? What good could possibly come from that level of anxiety? I would have stayed away, except for this one little problem. I knew deep inside, that God's desire was for me to keep trying.

I was taught as a child that when God gifts you with a talent, He doesn't intend for you to hide it, but rather share it with others in order to show His beauty and glory to the world. And, I agreed with that. Why have a gift or talent that you keep locked up inside your house, or your heart? What good can come from hoarding joy? But even if you know you should share your gifts, it doesn't make it easier to do it.

The truth I discovered was that I was angry with God—I felt as if I was doomed. No matter how many times I had asked Him to take away my fear, it seemed as if He didn't care. Ten years is a very long time to feel as frightened as I did. I believed that He could single handedly rescue me from my stage fright. He could bolster my bravery if He wanted to. I knew He could fix it all in an instant. And yet, He wouldn't do it for me. Every time I would enter the stage, especially when music was concerned, I would be flooded with feelings of hopelessness. "Why won't You take this away from me?" I would yell at the sky. My desire was to bring glory to Him. My motives were pure. I had nothing to gain, except the ability to serve Him with freedom.

I could sense that something was happening in my heart and mind that was blocking me from just letting go in worship. I knew I was choosing fear over faith in these moments, and I was limiting God's ability to live through me. I was lying to myself ... telling my mind that I couldn't do it, even though God had proven time after time that He could do it through me.

I can remember wondering what I possibly needed to learn from those frightening moments.

I knew I was miserable, and felt that my emotions indicated I was living outside of my strengths. Once again, because something didn't feel good, I wanted to run away. I didn't have an answer. But, one thing I did know was that I was angry and wanted deliverance.

That deliverance came in the form of counseling … you know, that exercise I had refused to participate in. And, to be completely honest with you, my fear of the stage did not leave right away. It took a great deal of therapy and prayers to bring me to a place of freedom.

When I finally did break down and enter into the process of rooting out my fears, I learned my intense anxiety had a beginning. I learned that getting over my fear would take willingness on my part to lean into the emotional reaction I had on stage and discover the reason behind it. Even the simplest of fears have a root cause. There are memories that live far beneath the surface, popping up only when summoned by similar trigger emotions. In counseling, I was encouraged to name those emotions. To feel every single one, and think about times in my life when I felt similar. Each terrifying emotion pointed back to a time of fear from the past.

One such memory that popped up during therapy was an embarrassing one I'd rather have forgotten. It involved a time when I had the opportunity to travel for my college and sing in a public relations group.

I had been having a good time, traveling from city to city, representing my school. I was among friends, and my eighteen year old self was enjoying a small taste of freedom. I typically had no problem standing on the stage night after night, sharing my voice with the crowd. I loved sharing truth from God's Word in the songs; I had a purpose and it was a wonderful experience.

One evening, on our way to the location, we were running late, and had the misfortune of getting lost. We meandered through wrong turn after wrong turn, until we finally arrived at our destination. We were so late, that the congregation was already seated in the small church. I will never forget the embarrassment that followed. We had no choice but to walk up the center aisle and begin setting up our sound equipment in front of the onlookers.

We were stressed, out of breath, and as I remember, glistening with beads of sweat. This was not the perfect way to make a good first impression. About half way through our time of singing, the room took on a slightly different aura. I started feeling a cloud of confusion in my head. I couldn't make my eyes focus on the people in the room, as they were beginning to get hazy. I tried to figure out why I was having this reaction. Yes, I was embarrassed and annoyed at the whole situation, but of all the things I should be feeling … dizzy wasn't one of them.

I gulped down a few breaths, and tried to calm my racing heart. I wanted to run out of that church. I wanted nothing to do with anything that was happening that night. I needed to escape. I needed to be anywhere but the middle of that stage.

When recounting that situation to my counselor, the words that came to mind were "trapped," "scared," "less than." The emotions I felt were worry, dread and confusion. What was fascinating to me is that those feelings were the same ones I would have when sharing on a platform fifteen years later. In fact, as time went on, every time I would think about the stage, I would have a visceral response. I wanted nothing to do with it, and yet I knew that I was capable of sharing the talents God had given me, and I even felt a degree of responsibility to do it. For the most part, I learned to battle through every time I needed to "perform." I was terrified and wounded by all the raging emotions, but I was resolved to win each time I was called. These raging emotions had a root cause. I didn't realize how much I was being affected by a much scarier moment in my past.

Allow me to take you back almost thirty years. The armed robbery that took place when I was a young child did much damage to my psyche. The trauma my family experienced was not only frightening, but also wreaked havoc on my ability to handle stressful situations. I didn't understand that my childhood experience was the underlying reason for my intense stress.

Any amount of fear would immediately send my mind into panic mode, where my brain was hijacked from any idea of rational thought. I thought I was crazy. I imagined I must be weak. I felt like a failure.

The truth was, every time I felt that trigger, it took me back to the time, which is to this day, the scariest moment of my life. I was a little girl, scarred by the trauma of gun-wielding masked men. I felt abandoned and afraid. The normalcy of my life was shattered by the evil desires of another person. I can still feel the cold sweat of fear that rose on my forehead as I woke to see a masked man holding my Dad hostage with a firearm. I could see their forms in the hallway, blocking my door. I felt confused, scared and alone. My protector could no longer protect me. The moments that followed were terrorizing as we ran for our lives. We wondered where they had taken my father and if we would ever see him again. I can still feel the sharp rocks under my feet as we ran into the bush. Shoes were left behind as we ran for cover.

That night ended well. While we emerged with less earthly possessions, my dad was mercifully released. As I drifted to sleep in the early hours of the morning, it was with a shattered sense of safety and a gnawing pain in the pit of my stomach. I was a frightened little girl who would experience new reactions to the smallest of fears. That little girl may have grown up on the outside, but the intense terror remained deep inside, waiting for triggers to call it out again.

I discovered that my deepest need in the moments following this trauma was to be held. I had just gone through the terrifying reality of having my dad taken as well as the huge adrenaline spike that came from the overall experience. I needed the warm feeling of safety to calm me down and let me know everything would work out. In the commotion and confusion of the night, that need was unintentionally overlooked.

As a thirty-something adult, I discovered that when I was on a stage, I desperately needed that same feeling of warmth and comfort. I needed to be held by a loving Father. For reasons that are beyond my understanding, the stage represented a trapped feeling for me. It would bring up the same emotions that were felt by my eight year old self on that fateful night.

In order to find freedom from those feelings of terror, I had to experience them again, and learn how to calm myself down in the moments when they surfaced. That welcomed relief came because of two things.

First, I wouldn't have been able to understand the nuances of my trauma if I had not been vulnerable and allowed a trained counselor to guide me through it. For those of you who are frightened to let someone help you in this area, please listen carefully: You have to let your skeptical assumptions go. I wish desperately that more people would trust the process of sound counseling. It is not a space where you cry a little and feel better. True healing happens in those rooms where people have dedicated their life to helping people find the root cause of their difficulty, whatever it may be.

Secondly, I had to lean into the gracious kindness of my heavenly Father. I had to believe that He will never leave or forsake me. He had to be enough in the moments when I was frightened. So much of my life had been about performance. And, while this had nothing to do with the trauma I experienced, my need to perform perfectly and my fear that I was not loved and held were morphing together in a confusing distraction. I wanted to be rid of that distraction and get up on whatever stage greeted me with a strong sense of who God had created me to be. I didn't need to perform. I didn't need to be anything more than me—the one He created on purpose. I had to come to the place where I would give my talent to Him, confident in my preparation, determined to give it my all, but reliant on His ability to hold me through it.

Practice makes perfect in some cases, but I'm not waiting for perfection anyway. Now, when I climb the stairs to what was once a scary stage, I remind myself that I am being *held*. I am being *carried* by the strength of my Creator, who knit me together in my mother's womb, and is aware of every moment that will fill my life. It doesn't have to turn out perfectly. My voice can break, and my fingers can slip off the keys. It doesn't matter.

I no longer need to allow that trauma to hijack simple moments of apprehension. The familiar twinge of nervousness in the pit of my stomach doesn't need to send me to a place of unbridled panic. I make the choice to worship unhindered, for only one purpose. To bring glory to God. I share my talents because I choose to. I'm not forced. I'm not coerced. I am not trapped. A loving God has gifted me with something beautiful to share with the world, and I am going to share it.

I can breathe in the beautiful grace that fills my life with purpose. He called me. He who called me will be faithful. He will walk beside me. He will cover me with his protection.

I love the verse in Psalm 91 that says, "This I declare about the LORD: He alone is my refuge, my place of safety; he is my God, and I trust him." (Psalm 91:2 NLT) I can name my fears. Speak my emotions. And rest in a God of safety.

Even when I don't feel safe in my surroundings, I have a loving God who is my place of safety. When the stage of my life is scary, as it will inevitably be, I can trust that the purpose I have been called to is more important than the temptation I am met with.

God would not have brought me here, if it wasn't for a purpose. He is shaping each one of us who have answered His call. We are the ones who carry His glory to the world. We are the ones that show His love to a world that longs for it. If we always give into the fear that tries to stop us, we will never arrive at the place God wants to take us to.

The fear still comes on days I'm asked to share my gifts, but I have learned to meet it face to face. I'm still learning to be brave. There are moments when I don't feel strong enough. There are many times when I would like to run away from the seemingly "big" thing God is asking me to do. I've even had good, well-meaning people tell me that it shouldn't be difficult to do God's will. That if I have that much trouble, it must mean that I am not in the ministry or spot that makes sense for me. While I understand their intention and the logic behind it, I've not experienced that in my own life. Music makes sense to me, but the sharing of that art has been a challenge. In the sharing of my gift, God has shaped me into the musician He wanted me to be. The fear of man—the terror of performance has threatened to take away my voice; and yet, I choose to stand up and fight for what I know God has gifted me to share.

I'm thankful for the people who have encouraged me to keep sharing—Those who have prayed with me before a church service. Those who have looked me in the eye and whispered truth to my frightened mind right before I went out to lead worship. If it wasn't for the people God put around me to lift me up, I wouldn't have the text messages from people who have been touched and inspired by what God has done through me. I wouldn't have the immense honor of sharing the victories that have been won with people who think they can't keep going. What an incredible joy it is to be able to grow from the moments that tempted me to flee in fear.

I've learned so much from that once scary stage.

I've discovered that it's not fearless people who are brave.

That title is reserved for those who are scared to death, but are stepping out to do it anyway.

Journal Exercise

Is there anything holding you back from
sharing your gifts with the world?
Think back to your childhood. Are there situations
you need to discuss with a licensed Counselor?

_____

_____

_____

_____

_____

_____

_____

_____

_____

_____

_____

"Some people feel guilty about their anxieties and regard them as a defect of faith. I don't agree at all. They are afflictions, not sins. Like all afflictions, they are, if we can so take them, our share in the Passion of Christ"

— *C.S. Lewis*

8

Stepping out of Safety to Serve

Who likes the comfort zone?

Well, if no one else will admit it, I will. I kind of like it. For most of my life I've preferred staying in my own corner—feeling calm, happy and unbothered.

It's not that I don't like to take care of others. On the contrary; I've enjoyed caring for people my entire life. It's one of the reasons I went to Nursing School. I was determined to make people feel better. To offer hope to the hopeless and silence the cries of the sick with the comfort I had to offer. I would come home from work giddy with excitement on days when I had discharged a patient in better shape than when I had received them.

But, If I'm honest, I typically like to make people feel better on my terms. If I feel comfortable in my surroundings, I do an excellent job caring for your needs. As soon as I feel anxiety and trepidation, I tend to become the one who needs care and assistance. I'm thankful to report that I have grown in this area and have learned to care for others within healthy boundaries. However, for many years I stayed well within my comfort zone to protect myself from being overwhelmed.

Perhaps that's why I found myself being careful of what I said yes to. I actually agreed to do a lot of jobs, ministries, and met many needs. But I typically said yes to the positions that involved me hunkering down scrubbing a toilet, or hiding in a back room doing something out of sight of most of the human race. I just felt better when my heart rate didn't increase, and where sweat drops could be discreetly wiped off without notice.

What can I say? I'm a typical introvert. I like people, and I can be friendly when needed, but if you require too much of me, or my tank is empty ... watch out. I become the quieter, more thoughtful version of myself, and that version hasn't always been so fabulous out in the front lines of ministry projects.

I'm so thankful that God has room for different personalities in His work. It takes literally all kinds of people to get the job done. And, for the most part, it seems that He places people in areas where they can shine. However, sometimes, as was the case of say, Moses, or David, He calls people who are emotional and scared to death to do really big things for Him.

I've decided that perhaps He decides to often use people who are terrified because He gets the glory when those people are effective. Many of our biblical heroes were stretched to their limit while doing great things for God. ("That's why I take pleasure in my weaknesses, and in the insults, hardships, persecutions, and troubles that I suffer for Christ. For when I am weak, then I am strong." II Cor. 12:10 NLT)

Let's look at Moses, for example. If you have a background in church life, you know a little about Moses. He was an Old Testament hero. He led the Hebrew people out of slavery from the Egyptians and was an effective leader for a long time. He listened to the advice of his father-in-law and appointed people to be in charge of groups, and delegated tasks to people who were better suited for the job. This ability to see potential and empower people is one of the qualities that marked him as a powerful leader.

But, the thing you have to understand about Moses, if you don't already, is that he had some significant weaknesses. In his early life, he not only had a temper, but he couldn't stand to do public speaking (I can identify with that part of his life)! Just as Moses had to learn how to leverage his strengths and delegate his weaknesses, we have to do the same. To do this, you *have* to know your strengths. Once you figure that out, you know which areas are more suited to your makeup. And, you can work on improving yourself in the areas where you are less inclined. This is not to say that we won't be asked to do things that fall in the category of our weaknesses. On the contrary; I believe God can help us to rise above those things that we aren't naturally good at and use us in ways we never dreamed. However, it is enlightening to understand your wiring. I'll never forget the first time I got a good look at what I was gifted in. Suddenly so many things in my life made sense. I understood who I was and the ways I could easily have a positive impact on the world around me.

As far as weaknesses go, it's important to come to terms with the tasks you don't do well. It's okay. It's not the end of the world.

You are not less important because you struggle with those areas. Knowing these areas gives you the unique opportunity to work with others who do have those strengths. Those involved in teams have the chance to become a beautiful arrangement of varying strengths all for the fame and glory of God.

I believe it's important however, that we not view our personality as a weakness. In my case, I am an introvert. There have been many times over the years that I've allowed my personality to frustrate me. I wanted to be something that I wasn't. To make matters more complicated, I have always been friendly. I can be outgoing when I need to be, so I don't fit the stereotypical mold of an introvert. There were many occasions when I came to the conclusion that something must be wrong with me, because I didn't handle certain situations well. My personality type had never been much of an issue until I struggled with anxiety. Introverts need space. They need time to recharge and reflect during their day. People who struggle with anxiety need a lot of time to recharge as well. Because of that, I have had to learn to create white space in my calendar. I typically make sure I have the time to recharge. There is absolutely nothing wrong with this. I had to get to the place where I came to terms with the way I was made. It made all the difference. I knew I had certain abilities, but was struggling through my commitments with difficulty. That was because I wasn't tending my emotional health—quite frankly, I didn't even know I needed to. Until I discovered more details about how I was wired, I didn't know what needed to be worked on and worked around. That is not an excuse to neglect self-improvement. I continue to push myself to be the most "extroverted-introvert" I can be. The reason I do that is because it is essential to the ministries and tasks I am typically involved in.

You may be frustrated with how you are wired. If you struggle with mental health issues, your personality may contribute negatively to your anxiety or depression. I know how you feel. It's frustrating to have a desire to get out there and do something, and feel like you are being held back by who you are!

I'd like to offer you some suggestions that could be helpful to your freedom. These steps can help you get past what is potentially holding you back. First of all, I'll say it again and risk overstating: Schedule an appointment with a good Counselor. There is no shame in admitting you need someone to help you sift through your wrong thinking, and figure out the root cause. For many of us, our anxiety is a result of a life-altering moment when we were young, or a bunch of small traumas that we have been through.

When I finally broke down and started seeing a licensed Counselor, everything changed. It was one of the most difficult things I have ever done, because the pain involved with uprooting years of fear was no joke. But, I am thankful for the results I see in my life because I finally put my mental health as a top priority.

She helped me to see the correlation between trauma I experienced as a young child during our robbery, to the anxiety I was dealing with as an adult. Emotions are tricky things. You might be tempted to believe that once a traumatic event is over, you should be fine. This is simply not true. When you haven't healed correctly from trauma, the damage can be continual. You must deal with the original event before you can move on to a place of freedom from that fear. In my case, every time I experienced another frightening experience, no matter how small, I went back to that terrifying night. I would ask my Counselor, "Why is this a big deal? Why is this bothering me? It doesn't seem to bother other people!" I didn't understand at that time that it's impossible to compare our responses to fear with how others react. We are all wired differently and have had a wide range of experiences. In my case, I was being traumatized every time something happened that activated a fear response. Because I had never healed from that event, I was dealing with a perpetual reminder of it.

Part of that is because I am incredibly empathetic by nature. I could see a story on the news or watch a commercial and be completely undone. I hadn't learned how to channel my empathy correctly. It would take over me until I no longer had control on how it affected me. If someone had a frightening experience, I was placing myself in their shoes—feeling their pain, even if I didn't know them. I could attend a funeral where I didn't know one person and be wrecked emotionally. It was a very unhealthy place to be, but I didn't understand the reason behind it.

I'll never forget sitting in her office, talking about my severe stage fright, and learning that the root cause was that dark African night when everything changed. The visceral feeling of fear. Seeing the masked man holding a gun to my Dad's head and feeling trapped. Fleeing into the bush and feeling the overwhelming desire to scream. Shaking with anxiety after my Dad was safely returned, because I couldn't stop the feeling that someone would take me away from the comfort I needed. God may have been near that night, but for some reason I didn't feel Him.

After that, when other tragedies would happen, I was immediately transported to the place where my feeling of safety and security was destroyed. After years of this cycle happening more times than I could count, my mind was incorrectly processing any kind of sad or frightening emotion.

When I would step out of my comfort zone as an adult, I would feel that normal human response to fear, and without knowing it, my mind was taking me to the moment I had experienced significant trauma. You don't have to tell your mind to go into fight or flight mode. It will do that all on its own.

Weeping through my story to a licensed Counselor seemed silly at the time, and now I realize it was the catalyst for my healing. She was able to help me know what I needed to do to heal those connections.

I told the story to my husband, as he held me safe. I recounted the story to my Mom, while she was visiting, and she held me with tears pouring down. She didn't know—I didn't even know—how traumatized I was as a young child.

I am convinced that God orchestrated the timing of my Mom's visit for my healing. The very week I was working on that part of my "counseling homework," she was visiting. The very person I needed to hold me safe as a child, was there as an adult while my mind was being healed. I felt the calming reassurance that everything would be okay. There we were, many years later, telling the little girl that she was safe … she was loved … she was held. As we held onto each other and wept, a loving God was holding us too. This was not a coincidence. This was miraculous healing that involved time and process. This healing would have never happened without a decision to get help.

Some of you may not have significant trauma to find healing from, but you may understand that you aren't willing to get out of your comfort zone. Perhaps it bothers you that you experience difficulty putting your fears aside to be part of something bigger than yourself.

Healing is vital, but once you have found some help for your pain, it's important to move to the next step. Walk in freedom. Emerge from the shadows of your hiding place and use the gifts that God has given you. Find a person who is trained in life coaching. Explore good websites which provide insight into who you are. There are so many people who can help you utilize your strengths. Talk to someone who is knowledgeable in that area, and seek their counsel. Don't sit on your gifts; they were designed to share.

As I look back on situations over the course of my teenage and adult life, I can see how I could have reacted differently if I had understood who I was, and how my mind worked. As a highly emotional person, I see the world in broad strokes of brilliant color. That view of the world taints experiences I have. At times I am tempted to believe the emotion I am feeling is the truth. In the past I have leaned towards putting too much emphasis on feelings. It wasn't necessarily God telling me think certain things. But, I thought it was, because of how I *felt*. Once you know the truth about how you are wired, you can weed through moments of confusion a little bit easier.

Lastly, I would say that the key to experiencing freedom is to just do the thing that scares you. It will feel counterintuitive. But, start small. Make little things that frighten you go away by conquering them.

This is not necessarily a call for bungee jumping and skydiving, but if it helps ... go for it! Rather, this is about stepping out of your comfort zone to help and encourage others even if it terrifies you. Maybe someone looks like they need a hug and a hello. You may be an introvert and the shyest person you know. Do it anyway. Walk over to that person, say the words, "you look like you could use a hug today," and encourage their lonely heart.

In my experience, I had to step out in small ways before I could walk with confidence into the situations that terrified me. It often felt like my world was crashing all around me, and that there was no way I could rise up from the ashes. But that was a lie. The truth was every time I said yes to the small adventure, I became braver than the moments before.

These days, when something frightens me, I feel as if I've been given a dare! I refuse to be held back. I will find a way. I may not do it perfectly, and it may take some time, but I don't believe in giving up.

Not too long ago, someone asked me what one word I would use to describe myself, and without a second thought, the word that came to mind was "fierce." I almost couldn't believe that it came to my mind so quickly! Me? Fierce?

And yet, here I am. I'm fierce. I've always been that emotionally charged, purpose driven, sassy introvert who wanted to change the world. I just hit some speed bumps along the way.

You too, may just now be aware that underneath all the fear and anxiety is a heart and soul ready to move. You are sick of letting your emotions take you places you never wanted to go. You might be looking at a big task in front of you, a job that seems overwhelming, a ministry that you feel ill-equipped for. Look at it with fierce eyes and don't back down.

Step out of your safety zone. Franklin D. Roosevelt famously said the "only thing we have to fear is fear itself."

I'm giving you permission to stop fearing your fears. They don't have to define you. Those fears are nothing compared to the strength that lives just below the surface—daring you to live the life you were created for.

Step out of the safety zone, armed with what you know and determined to find out what you don't. If it scares you—too bad— Your fear doesn't get to call the shots. Get out there and do what you were made to do.

Journal Exercise

What is one thing you wish you could
change about yourself, and why?
Challenge yourself to see that trait in a different way. How
might the world become better because of how you are designed?
Are there areas of weakness in which you need to improve?

_____

_____

_____

_____

_____

_____

_____

_____

_____

_____

"As you walk through the valley of the unknown, you will find the footprints of Jesus both in front of you and beside you."

- Charles Stanley

9
Walking with Women

With every fear that I challenged, another one would approach me and threaten to steal whatever victory I had gained. I became aware I needed to take each fear down with a power greater than me. I began to sense that God was calling me to walk paths I had previously been avoiding.

I have this fabulous mentor in my life who, to this day encourages me to be all I can be. She has high hopes for me, and won't let me forget it! One day she pitched the idea of me leading a women's Bible Study. I kind of laughed and shrugged it off. I wasn't really interested and it made my stomach churn at the thought. I was intrigued by the idea of helping people learn truths from God's Word, in fact I'm a teacher at heart. However, I didn't feel equipped to effectively handle my anxiety. At point I hadn't started counseling and I hadn't faced up to my dread of the unknown. My sweet friend would not be dissuaded. She arrived at church one day, book in hand, and asked me to consider leading it. I told her I would take it home and pray about it.

If I wanted to stay in my safety zone, I should have put up a bigger fight that day. I started reading the book, and knew I had to help share it with others. It was, "The Best Yes," by Lysa Terkeurst. How fitting for one of my biggest ventures out of the dark. It was almost like a metaphor of my struggle. I was transitioning from a place of saying no to everything I thought I wasn't strong enough to do to saying yes to God's beautiful leading. I didn't know at that time that He was leading me to minister to people. This introvert would have much preferred staying home in her little comfort zone and calling it a day. Wouldn't you know it, that life was not meant to be. I felt a stirring that I couldn't ignore, so I said yes to a new way of life.

I led that study with fear and trembling. There were several ladies older than me—I mean several. Who was I to be leading them? Thank God they had grace for a young pastor's wife who shuddered at the thought of serving in that way. The experience of teaching stretched me in ways that were both frightening and exhilarating.

That study became one of the biggest moments for me in emerging from the shadows. I had always preferred staying in the background. And now it was obvious that God wanted me to get up from my ministry of merely scrubbing toilets and wiping snotty noses to a platform that included public exhortation. Yes, it seemed that God actually wanted me to speak to a room full of people!

I had some fascinating experiences that first year of teaching. Experiences that challenged and stretched me. I not only had to face my angst of getting up in front of people, but I had to study more than I ever had in order to learn and grow as a teacher.

If you want to know one of the quickest ways to enlarge your comfort zone, say yes to teaching people who know more than you. The emotional stress isn't fun, but the knowledge you acquire trying not to look stupid is fabulous.

Such was my experience. I wanted to be taken seriously, at least a little; so I pushed harder than I ever had before. I was reading commentaries, perusing multiple articles a day, and watching YouTube tutorials about how to be a better speaker. I was determined to grow as a Bible study leader. I refused to be mediocre, even if my hands trembled and my knees knocked every time I stood up to the podium. I knew I might not be talented in the area of public speaking, but I was determined to be as good as I could be.

I remember one such occasion. I entered a room full of women, determined to allow them to see a confident leader. Little did I know that I was about to encounter one of the most unnerving situations of my ministry life. Someone challenged me in a shocking manner. Without going into details it was an absolutely disturbing situation. My heart raced, my palms turned sweaty, and I had a host of eyes staring at me, wondering how I would handle this person. I did the only thing I knew to do at that moment … I cried out silently to God. I begged Him to give me strength to answer this woman in a respectful and loving way.

Thankfully I had been taught that defending truth is important, but also that how you defend it is just as important. It can be difficult to stand up for weighty matters, especially when you hate confrontation and feel incredibly insecure in your position. And yet, I found myself in a predicament. I could either let it go, and move on, or I could say what needed to be said with the boldness of the Holy Spirit.

I chose the latter, and I have to say that at the end of that study, I emerged a tiny bit stronger. I felt limp from the confrontation, and had no interest in repeating the scenario. Truth be told, I would be forced to repeat it several times that year, and each time I would cry out to God for help. Let me assure you, He most certainly showed up every single time.

Those experiences have taught me so much about bravery. I have come to believe that we can't be brave unless we are engaging in activities that scare us. If we live secluded from the world, without any inclination to step out of our safety net, we won't be forced to learn how to handle conflict. We won't learn how to get back up and try again when we fail. And, we won't learn what it means to rely on something ... *Someone* greater than ourselves in moments when we would rather run away.

We must fight through the fear. And when we find that our bravery is lacking, we must lean into the apprehension to learn from the process. A special kind of tenacity becomes normal as we grow through uneasy situations.

Not long after I started leading Bible studies, I felt a stirring within me to host a special evening for the ladies in our church—A special event for women. When I approached our pastor about the concept, he was excited about it, and wanted me to go for it. In all honesty, I didn't really know what I was doing, but I was determined to obey what I felt God was asking me to do.

We called the evening, "In Focus." It was an evening designed to help the women in our community get their eyes focused on the right things in life. We had great worship, an engaging speaker, and worthy causes to get behind as a group. It was a fabulous evening, and I sat down with the satisfaction that I had obeyed God's leading, and that it had gone so well. I had no expectations that anything would follow.

Our pastor let me know that he wanted to meet for a discussion about the event. When I sat down in his office, I had no idea what was about to happen. He informed me that he wanted me to do the event again. He felt that I couldn't just do one event and quit. I needed to continue with this idea, and see what happened. That is not what I had planned.

I couldn't easily refuse, so I nodded begrudgingly, and agreed to work on planning another event. I dove into continuing with the vision of helping women adjust their perspective towards what was important.

Two events later, I found myself in that same office, having a discussion about what was next. I didn't know what was to come, but my pastor encouraged me to look to God for direction about what should happen with this opportunity.

I began to pray and research ideas. I combed through websites for inspiration. I looked to Scripture for guidance on what a purposeful ministry for women could look like. I approached the team of ladies who had helped me pull off the events, and we prayed for wisdom.

Then one day, the lightbulb moment happened. I knew without a doubt which direction we should go. I had vision. I had purpose. I had a calling to make this ministry a reality, rather than an impromptu rendezvous. Now, this experience was fascinating and confusing at the same time, because I had never wanted to be involved in any kind of women's ministry. It was intimidating to say the least.

During this time of strategizing, I came across an invitation to attend a Beth Moore conference, with the option of participating in You Lead, which is a training seminar for women in ministry. I brushed it aside in my mind, but mentioned it in passing to my husband, Brian.

He strongly encouraged me to go, and made it work with the budget so that I could purchase a ticket. I wanted to run from the opportunity. I wasn't comfortable in settings like that. I would much rather stay in my comfortable house and watch tutorials on YouTube. At that point in my journey, I still dealt with feelings of discomfort any time I was in a room with a lot of people and had to adhere to a program. And because it was geared towards women who ministered in their church, I told myself it didn't apply to me.

I had this major problem with being called a "Women's Leader." I didn't want to be associated with that title, especially when it involved being part of a church. I wanted to lead an organization that helped and inspired women and our community, but I wanted to do it on my own. I didn't want to be the church women's leader. It's amusing to me now, but I took issue with titles like that. It spoke of pressure and expectation to me, and I wanted no part of that. I also had a serious problem with accountability. I wanted to be able to go rogue … quitting anytime I felt like it. I'm so glad God kept drawing me, coaching me into becoming transformed in this area.

The day came for the training, and I nervously checked in, feeling out of place and out of sorts. I was excited to learn, and yet kept wondering if I was in the right place. I even called Brian and lamented over the phone, "I just wish I could have some kind of confirmation that I'm on the right track." I was about to get that confirmation.

During a break between sessions, I ran to the ladies' room. Upon exiting I began talking to the leader of the training. She was a kind woman and we enjoyed chatting for a few minutes. When she inquired about where I was from and what church I was affiliated with, I started to tell her the vision I felt God had given me. We only had a short time to talk, as it was time for her session. It happened to be the one I would be attending, so I followed her into the room and found my seat.

She began to speak and at one point was discussing different ministry models. She turned to me and said, "Would you mind sharing what you are doing in this area?" My mouth went dry and my knees knocked, but I rose to my feet and found the words to tell the room full of women what God had been leading me to do. I told them about our desire to have an organization for Christian women in the area that focused on learning about God and loving others.

No sooner had I sat down, than someone beside me handed me a note. It was from a gal down the row who wanted to connect with me. As soon as the session was over, she ran over to me with such excitement that you could feel it from yards away. I found myself being introduced to the women who was in charge of coordinating the event for that city. The statement that came out of her mouth made no sense to me, but I listened all the same. "We've been praying for you!" she kept exclaiming over and over.

I must have looked stunned and confused, because she began to explain that she was part of a group of women in the area who had been meeting together and would soon be disbanding. She said they had been praying about it, and had felt strongly that God was raising someone up to lead women in this area.

Now, the truth is, I may not be the *one* God was raising up in that capacity, but that didn't matter. What mattered is that I had been searching for confirmation that I was on the right track, and God showed me that I was, in the most obvious way possible.

It was exactly what I needed. The next year would prove trying and confusing in many ways and I would question my calling. I would assume that I wasn't the person for the position. One of those times came during a Leader's Retreat put on by our church. We took a test that would reveal our personality/gifting. The result I got was not one that would be conducive to leading a large group of people.

The leader, one of my mentors, took one look at my results, put her arm around me and said, "We will be praying for you." I wasn't sure exactly how to take that, but I knew I must have a big challenge in front of me. That challenge would grow into my accepting the position of Women's Director at the church. The very thing I said I would never do—the accountability I thought I didn't want—became a reality. I won't get into all that God has led me to do as a result of that decision. But, I will tell you that I have been stretched in so many ways because of my obedience.

In all of the ups and down, God has led me. He took me from a "best yes," leading a Bible Study, to leading a women's event, to starting a ministry that was scary and wonderful all at the same time, to doing the thing I never wanted to do—minister to women.

It's all come to fruition by taking one step of obedience at a time. It was a walk into the unknown that required blind faith, and encouraged me more than I could have ever imagined. Through my experience as a ministry leader, I have grown in remarkable ways. I've come to love encouraging women in their lives—helping them to learn dependence on God. I've learned important lessons and been stretched in crucial ways that have led to the development of my character. I've learned how vital accountability is to success. I've learned how to lead with integrity and intention. I've learned how to stand up in the front of a room without wanting to run away. And I learned that by sticking to it and saying yes.

The very thing you can't imagine doing might be the thing that helps you grow the most. Say yes to the question that frightens you. Push past the fear and walk into a life of bravery that looks more like plain old obedience during mundane life.

I can tell you with confidence ... God will show up.

Journal Exercise

Talk about a time when you allowed apprehension to keep
you from saying yes to an opportunity for growth.

_____

_____

_____

_____

_____

_____

_____

_____

_____

_____

_____

"I am no longer anxious about anything, as I realize the Lord is able to carry out His will, and His will is mine. It makes no matter where He places me, or how. That is rather for Him to consider than for me; for in the easiest positions He must give me His grace, and in the most difficult, His grace is sufficient."

- Hudson Taylor

10

When Callings Collide

I mentioned briefly how confused I was during the time I was starting "In Focus," the women's organization with a surprising start. There were a couple of reasons for that. One, I tend to be a Pleaser. I'm a people pleaser, I'm a friend pleaser, I'm a God pleaser. Disappointing someone in any of those categories is one of my worst fears. And disappointing God definitely tops the list.

I've grown up with the unreasonable fear that I will accidentally go down the wrong path and that God will discard of me because of my unworthiness. I want to know every minute of every day that I'm in the correct lane on the path towards my destiny. Yep, that's been my struggle.

Because of this propensity towards God-pleasing perfectionism, I found myself constantly questioning whether I was involved in the right activities. I wanted to be sure that I was focused on the correct "calling," if you will. I counted my positions as a wife and a mother to be paramount. But, after that I encountered confusion about the passions and desires I felt within my inner being.

This has been my life:

I am a wife. A ministry wife. There probably shouldn't be any expectations on those of us in this position, but let's face it, there just are. We are women who have followed our husbands to a place of sacrifice. We don't pick this position for the money, fame or good times. We exist in this space for the saving and guidance of hurting people.

I love music. When I hear the swelling sound of an orchestra, I am moved to tears. I close my eyes and take in the beauty that exudes from the instruments. When I play the piano and sing in the comfort of my living room, I am whisked away to another place. There are few moments in my day that don't involve some kind of tune playing in my mind. I speak the language of music, and can't imagine life without it.

I am a creative. I adore photographing a special moment and editing it to the degree it speaks to me. I've tried my hand at designing children's clothes and accessories. My heart leaps at the thought of making something special. It's my own form of art, and I live for the spaces in time when I have the pleasure of creating.

I love to study. My world is not big enough. I have to know more ... learn more ... and share more. I am a teacher in the core of my being. I enjoy sharing the treasures I've learned with other people in order to make their lives better. When I know something, I have to tell someone, even if that person is my long-suffering husband who puts up with my impromptu lectures. If I could have my nose in a book or attend a class every other day, I would be thrilled.

I am a Mom. I love my kids and want to be involved in their school and their special activities. I want to provide a meaningful childhood for them to look back at with fondness. I want to make them nutritious meals and spend enough time with them individually so that they don't have to spend too much time on a therapist's couch (I kid). I'm absolutely humbled and honored at the idea that I get to raise world changers. I don't take that responsibility lightly.

I adore writing. There are so many words inside my mind, all jumbled up that beg to come out and inspire others. I have loved the written word my entire life. Whether in my journal or for a specific purpose, I am obsessed with the crafting of a sentence to portray a feeling, a moment, a life-changing perspective.

I am a friend. There are people with whom I love to spend time with, and reasons why those relationships must be cultivated. Friendship is a gift from God, and I believe healthy relationships reveal a great deal of beauty. I want to make a difference in the lives of those around me. I long to be an intentional friend who offers a safe place for people to come to.

My relationship to each one of these things/people are worthwhile and deserving of my time. However, doing all of them can take up a great deal of my day and must be prioritized in a purposeful way. I happen to believe that putting my husband and children first is the most important place to start. While I know that I am not excelling in this area every day, or even every week, it does enter my thought process often. I check in. I test the waters. I observe the emotional temperature of our home to see if I am needed in a greater capacity.

But, after I have made them my first priority, what then? How do I know which direction to head in at that point? When you have so many interests ... so many God-given passions, what happens then?

I grew up thinking that the medical field would have much of my time and energy. I imagined that my life as a nurse would be fulfilling and wonderful. I loved helping people. I found great fulfilment in walking with people to a place of wholeness. And yet, at the end of the day, my career as a nurse never took off, mostly because it wasn't the right fit for me (is this a good time to mention I don't like blood—No wonder that career never took off!) What I loved about nursing was that I was able to comfort people who were experiencing pain. As an empathizer, I was able to give them a different kind of care. I discovered that the medical field was not the arena I would spend my life in, but that didn't stop me from using my gifts in a caring way.

I find myself now as a creative in full time ministry who loves to walk alongside others in their journey. I am fulfilling what I thought I might be doing someday, just in a slightly different field. I am walking with people to a place of wholeness. I am investing in the health of the ones I share life with. I have come to understand that the health of one's soul is of great importance. I didn't always appreciate this calling. In fact, there were times I resented it, if I'm being honest. But, I have come to the place of full surrender—I am all in. There are few things I love more than encouraging my husband in his ministry and walking *beside* him in this life of service.

We are warriors, fighting beside each other for the same cause. We are in this spiritual battle together and nothing will stop what the Lord wants to do with us as a team.

I remember one particular night before I was to lead worship at church. I slept fitfully that night. I found myself dreaming about all my different passions and I awoke with a lot of confusion. It was as if my subconscious mind was trying to sort all the things that were taking my time and attention. My callings were colliding. In my state of sleep, bewilderment was trying to creep in. But it wasn't just during my dream state that I was experiencing confusion. I knew I had to make sense of this season of my life ... a season in which I had my hand in several worthy causes. That day, I had to wake up, give it to God, and wholeheartedly give myself to what I was called to in that moment. I had a sneaking suspicion that I needed to get some clarity about why I was feeling so overwhelmed by my different "callings."

A conversation I had with another ministry wife came to my mind during that time. I remember her describing her different roles at church. She was heavily involved in at least three different areas, and I remember thinking she must be crazy. How on earth could she stay sane with all those different responsibilities pulling in different directions, I wondered. Now, to be fair, her kids were older than mine, so comparing our situations was inapplicable at best. However, I was trying to understand how to juggle the various responsibilities, interests and passions with grace.

It's important to note that there are differing opinions on this subject. Some who claim to be experts will suggest that people should focus on one area for the greatest success. Others will disagree and advocate for a variety of passions. But, in all the reading and listening I have done, I have come away with one simple truth. Some things deserve first place in your attention. Others do not.

I've learned that there is never an easy answer to this question of what gets our time. Prioritization is important, but my frustration went deeper than that. There were a couple directions I could have gone at that particular moment—areas I could have focused on more than others. How was I to know which path to take? The anxiety I had dealt with for so long wasn't helping me make any decisions. I had been through too many years of being overwhelmed.

Some people are better at multi-tasking than others, and we have to be honest with ourselves whether or not we are capable of that special kind of ability. But, for many of us, we will do a variety of things during the course of our lives, and that leads us to question which step to take first. Should we do it all, or focus on one passion at a time? This can be especially confusing for people who are artistic by nature. There are typically a plethora of desires welling up in the hearts of those who long to create. And, in those who are conscientious, the longing to please God in everything we do can weigh heavily in our decision making. The beautiful truth is that all those passions can create a stunning symphony of service to God when they are surrendered to him.

There are, of course, times to say no. There are seasons of prioritization in which certain callings will be of first importance. But, more often than not, we will find ourselves with a variety of responsibilities and we must find a way to handle these various duties with grace. It's a delicate balance that we all have to figure out how to handle. And truthfully, I haven't met a lot of people who have mastered the art of "balance."

In my case, I had to learn to stop complaining about the different areas in my life that were vying for my attention. They weren't going away anytime soon. Instead of lamenting that "I had so much to do," I had to shape up and act like an adult. May I make some suggestions that have been helpful to me? If you aren't a multitasker, learn to be a better one. It may sound strange, but it's completely possible. If you struggle with handling all your engagements, invest in a good planner and write things down. If you need to say no to some unnecessary tasks, do it. Don't beat around the bush. Just say no. The important stuff gets to have a spot on your calendar—anything else can wait until you are free.

If you discover that you are drowning with the weight of presumed responsibility, go back to the drawing board and allow God to take the burden of it off your back. We so often assume that we have to do more than others and be the best at what we do in order to be "enough." He has already done the hard work. All we have to do is walk faithfully in what He has led us to in that moment. Allow that "feeling" of responsibility to fall off your shoulders and slip off your back onto the floor. Then leave it behind. I'm not advocating walking away from commitments you have made. We should honor our promises and stay true to our word. But rather, I would encourage you to shift your thinking if your life has become about performing, rather than resting in God's provision.

At one time, I had become overly performance motivated—doing things that I really didn't need to because I felt like I had to help God out. Our job is to do our best with the talents He has given us. If that means that we are using one of them at a time, that's great! If we are asked to stretch ourselves thin for a season of time, I believe He will sustain us. He will be faithful. It's not that we strive uselessly, but that we step faithfully. One at a time—Saying yes when He gently leads; using no when we sense Him asking us to wait.

I met with our pastor not long ago as I was trying to figure out which direction to go—which passion to focus on. His insight was so helpful to me, and I'd love to share it with you. He helped me to focus not on one particular avenue to walk down, but to examine what gifting united all of the pursuits I felt called to. I had been so focused on trying to make one thing work, which is almost impossible for a "creative." Pastor Keith was able to call out what he saw as the common denominator in all of my areas of ministry. As soon as we had that conversation, it was as if a light had turned on in my brain.

He encouraged me to give up the things that would hinder me in the gift God had given me and work on using that talent for the glory of God. It made so much sense. I had been looking at my life as a fragmented picture that I needed to disassemble and remake. That wasn't what I needed to do at all!

I discovered that it is possible to be a spouse, parent, friend, hold a job, lead a ministry, and care for others ... all at the same time. We are often called to all of those things. And somehow I had come to this idea that my life had to become singular in nature. That I must only be able to be a good mom and nothing else. Or good at my job, and nothing else. Or good at ministry, and nothing else. On the contrary! I had to learn to prioritize properly, ask for help when needed and give up my need to perform for good.

We tend to allow one thing to dominate our thoughts. To control us in ways that can be unhealthy. Even our children can become idols in our lives. We can put them above everything else and live our lives around them. We should allow nothing to control us but God alone. We must give Him the power over our schedule. We must give Him the permission to lead us in and out of seasons with grace.

If life has to be perfectly buttoned up with a beautiful bow on top, then it's probably not a realistic life. Walking in step with God's plan is often messy. There will be moments of confusion and chaos. It doesn't have to stay that way, but a little season of uncertainty never hurt anyone.

The most important thing you can do is to prioritize the answering of the question "What will you do with God?"

He is God.

He isn't an afterthought. He isn't an appointment you scribble in between the important ones.

He knew you before you were formed in your mother's womb (Jeremiah 1:5). That level of knowing deserves more than simple acknowledgement.

He. Must. Come. First.

I admit to you that I don't always work this out perfectly in my own life. I need grace every single minute of my life. But I can tell you the desire to know Him and to be used by Him is so great that it's palpable.

I John 2:3 says, "And we can be sure that we know him if we obey his commandments." (NLT) Do you feel a sense of urgency to follow His commands? Do you long for His grace? Do you seek His will?

If none of this sounds familiar, then perhaps it's time you started at the beginning. Are you sick and tired of demanding control? I implore you to give God the rightful place in your life. The place that grants the Sovereign God permission to tell you what to do.

If He created you to focus on one thing, then do that one thing to the glory of God. But, if you find yourself called to be a wife, mother, friend, encourager, ministry leader, (fill in the blank), do each of those things with purpose and passion. Allow God to flow through you and guide every step.

If the moment comes when you know God is leading you to step away from one thing to focus on the most important things, do it prayerfully and leave your desires at the door.

Self-care is one thing. Prioritizing self above all, including God is another. His timing is perfect, and His strength is enough. Don't allow fear to become an excuse to get what your flesh desires.

Sometimes our callings will feel overwhelming. We will wonder how we will get up the next day and do all He's called us to do. That's okay. I would venture to guess that every single person who has lived a life of purpose has felt overwhelmed from time to time. It's just part of the process. It's about growing, learning, and stretching to do things we thought were impossible.

More often than not, those things weren't possible without help from someone other than ourselves. We stand on the shoulders of those who have gone before us. We learn from other's mistakes, and from some of our own. We can't live a life of purpose without purposeful living.

In the moments when you feel overwhelmed in the purpose you have been created for, remember you are not alone. Every hero or heroin that we look up to felt they were not up to the task at one time or another. We are human. We were never meant to be God. We can't make it even one step further without His sustaining power.

So for those of us with mental health challenges, may we not count ourselves out before we even get started. We might look at the passions and desires that we have and wonder how on earth we can get it done. We might wonder if there is a way to live without feeling pressure every single day. We may be tempted to give up on the things we know we were created to do. But we can't.

If it weren't for a nervous man named Moses, the Israelites wouldn't have been freed. If it weren't for an emotional king named

David, we wouldn't know as much about the heart of God. If it weren't for an impulsive Peter, we wouldn't understand that God builds His church on imperfect people.

Our calling is not an accident. Even with our shortcomings and our failures, God wants to use us. Imperfect as we are, all He asks is that we wait upon Him and allow Him to renew our strength. To keep going when it feels impossible. To walk this journey of faith, letting Him take our burdens and take the credit. We can't do this on our own. But, why would we want to anyway?

Journal Exercise

What does your calendar/planner look like? Do you need to put "first things first," and let some things go? Or, are you struggling with laziness? What step can you take today to live a more purposeful life?

_____

_____

_____

_____

_____

_____

_____

_____

_____

_____

_____

"Dear brothers and sisters, when troubles of any kind come your way, consider it an opportunity for great joy. For you know that when your faith is tested, your endurance has a chance to grow.

James 1:2,3 (NLT)

11
Joy in the Journey

Remember how I said this was not the book I dreamed of writing? It goes deeper than that. My life hasn't been the one I thought I would be living. Don't get me wrong, I love my life. It has taken many twists and turns, but it has been full of love and adventure. But, I haven't done all the things I thought I would do by the age I am now. As a kid I had so many dreams, and I had an imagination bigger than you can fathom. I was always going to be a world changer. From my earliest memories, the sky was the limit. If I was scared of something big, I dreamed of the day it would no longer pose a threat to my intention of seeing it through.

You could imagine my surprise when the trajectory of my life veered off to a surprisingly different direction. I was stunned, disappointed and annoyed. As I mentioned, there were also some intense moments of anger. I felt as if I couldn't make my body do what I wanted it to. I had been created to love life and during my darkest days I couldn't imagine loving anything. It was a hard reality that I wanted to walk away from.

I can't say I ever contemplated ending my life, but I do remember thoughts coming to my mind at one point that declared the bleakness of my existence. I can recall thinking, "everyone would be better off without me." The most frightening thing to me now—while looking back—Is that no one would have guessed that. As I said, I was pretty good at keeping a mask on when I needed to. After years of what felt like never-ending mental blocks, I was frustrated and unhappy.

Perhaps God knew that I needed to learn some difficult lessons so that I could grow into the person He created me to be. If I'm honest, prior to my humbling bout with anxiety, I was a cocky character. I thought I had life figured out and I was pretty sure I knew what I was talking about most of the time. I had every reason to be happy because life was going pretty great. I had talent and determination; the world was mine.

"Just kidding!" It felt as if life's circumstances were yelling those words at me when everything began to crumble. I suddenly realized how big the world was, and how unprepared I was for the hurdles I was facing. It seemed like a cruel joke that the "good girl" who tried to do everything perfectly would be given this cross to bear.

God doesn't ask our opinion about which cross we would like to bear. We don't get a multiple choice question with the option to check the box with the hardship we'd like to endure. Part of being human involves pain, sacrifice and what I'd like to call "growth opportunities." God uses our experiences to teach us lessons about Him and to smooth out the rough edges in our lives. I know I had a lot of edges to even out—I still do! I have come to understand that this side of heaven will involve some pretty frustrating days and I can't expect perfection until I see Jesus face to face.

I believe the key to my healing has been two fold. I had to learn to accept the circumstances that had become my normal. If I struggle with anxiety for the rest of my life, God is still good. He hasn't changed and He will be faithful for me. I have to look forward—To the day when the trials of this life will be no more. Resting in that truth brings incredible comfort and confidence. The other part is that I've had to learn reliance on God. To trust that He is over all and will ultimately bring to pass what He desires. Not only do I believe that is true for this world, but for my life as well. I don't have to stress out about every little frustration that I am faced with because I know the One in charge of it all!

One of the exercises that has been the most helpful for me on my journey is what I call "reframing my thinking." There have been a couple of ways that I have focused my behavior in order to arrive at a different result than I had previously. Excessive fear and worry had taken over parts of my brain to such a degree that a simple conversation could turn into a dramatic episode. I would overthink everything that had been said and worry that I might have said something wrong. I would think about how the other person might be interpreting the opinions I had voiced. Would they still think of me in the same way? Was I representing myself well with the words I had chosen? Was I representing God well? It was exhausting.

One particular day, I was discussing some recent situations with my Counselor and was being particularly hard on myself. I was discussing all the things I could have done differently. I should have done this. I should have said that. You get the picture. I was putting myself down in such a negative way, that she finally put a stop to my rant. "Let me ask you a question," she said. "Would you speak the way you are about one of your closest friends?" I was stunned and thought back to what I had just been saying. I looked up at the ceiling and paused, weighing every word as if I knew life change was around the corner. "No," I replied softly. "No." My voice got louder. "I would never speak that way about one of my friends." "Then, why would you speak so harshly about yourself?" She asked. "I think you need to give yourself some grace."

That wasn't easy for me to do, but I left that day, thinking seriously about what had just occurred in that room. My incorrect thinking and toxic inner dialogue had just been exposed and I knew it needed to change. I knew one of the reasons for this bent toward negative self-talk; It was my never ending quest for perfectionism. I had the unfortunate inclination for seeing every situation through the lens of what it *could* be. I would end every discussion, event, job, etc and think about how much better I could have been. It was a vicious cycle and I knew I needed out of it.

Over the next few days, weeks and months, every time I would start to think negatively about myself or a situation, I would immediately stop and ask myself one simple question. "Would I say or think this about a friend of mine?" Most often, the answer was no. I would consciously halt that line of thinking and choose a positive spin on the situation to dwell on. This type of reframing has been incredibly helpful to me. I have changed my outlook just by thinking differently about my interactions with others as well as the manner in which I have completed tasks. Have I perfected this exercise? No. Far from it. However, when I sense a bent toward incorrect thinking, I now have a tool which I use to change my inner dialogue.

The other exercise that I have found immensely helpful is

memorizing and focusing on Scripture. During the time when I was tackling all my fear issues head on, it was suggested that I find key verses to meditate on during the day. I made some 3x5 cards, looked up my favorite verses on the things I was dealing with and made myself a stack of promises. Every day I would keep those cards near me. They went to town with me in my purse. I would pull them out at stoplights and read them again and again. I ended the evening with them by my bed, once again going over the truth I desperately needed to hear. Slowly but surely, those verses—the very words of God became etched on my heart. I pulled them out when I was particularly anxious. I repeated them out loud. I would quote them back to God in a prayer. "Now Lord, you say that You have not given me a spirit of fear. You have given me a spirit of power, love and a sound mind. I'm claiming that today!"

My life changed. My mind was transformed from the inside out. So much so that people would mention to me that something was different. They saw a different Jamie than they had known before. I was learning how to accept my humanness and was choosing to rely on God for strength.

It was tremendously helpful to look to Scripture for answers because of the example of the men and women in the Bible. I haven't found one example of an "easy life" in the Word of God. Have you? They all went through life with burdens, pain and suffering. I haven't seen any examples of blissful lives with absolute perfection. On the contrary, most of the people we read about went through hardship after hardship, and the only thing holding them up was their reliance on God. I particularly love the Psalms for that reason. David was such an honest voice when describing how he was feeling in the moment. There were really good days in which he was overwhelmed by the goodness of God. And then you read about other occasions in which David felt that he was almost swallowed by destruction. And yet, he wrote verses like this: "You are my God, and I will praise You; You are my God, I will exalt You. Oh, give thanks to the Lord, for He is good! For His mercy endures forever." (Psalm 118:28,29 NKJV)

The goodness of God is where I tended to get hung up. I was having a hard time believing God was good when I didn't feel good. I'm thankful for the examples I have seen before me of those who called God good even on bad days. They have inspired and challenged me to a new perspective. He is still a good Father when my life isn't paradise. If all He had done for me was die for my sins … it's enough. If all He had done for me was to rescue my soul from destruction … it's enough. He doesn't owe me anything and yet He gives me everything! When we cry, He answers. When we fail, He is faithful. When we break, He repairs our souls.

He is faith—when we are failing.

He is hope—when we are hurting.

He is love—and His love never fails. (Psalm 136)

He cannot be anything but faithful. We mess up all the time and He continues to lift us up out of the pits we put ourselves in. I may not have chosen anxiety as my thorn in the flesh, but the thorn is just part of being flesh! We are not divinity—we are human.

While I don't believe in chasing a life of unrealistic perfection, I do believe in the power of God that transforms a person from the inside out. We don't have to strive to make ourselves better because God does the work. We do, however play a part in our freedom. We have to accept the power that Christ offers us. When we have surrendered our lives to Him, we have the same power that raised Christ from the dead living inside of us. What strength we possess! So next time your fear whispers dread to your mind, square your shoulders back and shout your victory. "In all these things we are more than conquerors through him who loved us!" (Romans 8:37 ESV) This is something you'll have to declare more than once. With every victory comes another battle. I won't sugar coat it. Life is tough, but God is still good.

I've also had to learn to appreciate and accept the person God made me to be. I've struggled over the years, wishing I could be something I'm not. I imagined the perfect Jamie and wanted to achieve that version of me I idolized. I imagined that once I reached the pinnacle of my perfection life would suddenly be everything I wanted it to become. That's a lie. The person we are in this moment is enough. It doesn't mean we stay that way. It doesn't mean we don't strive for something better. But we must never tell ourselves that we aren't enough. We are enough when Christ lives in us. We are worthy when Christ makes us righteous through his sacrifice. Anything more we can do is meaningless in light of our salvation. We have to get to the place where we look in the mirror and declare that we will choose joy in spite of what looks back at us. That we will live in the power of the resurrected Lord. That we will get our eyes off temporary disappointments and get our vision fixed on how those disappointments can bring glory to God.

This life isn't about us. We can enjoy it. We can be thankful for the incredible blessings we have. But, we must always keep our perspective adjusted to the truth of God's word. "Rejoice in our confident hope. Be patient in trouble, and keep on praying." (Romans 12:12 NLT)

I don't want to be the girl that deals with anxiety. I don't want that to be my legacy. I want for God to work so powerfully in my life that when others see me they say, "That's the girl who rises above her afflictions with joy and brings glory to God through her circumstances."

That's a life worth living.

Journal Exercise

Do you have a habit of speaking negatively about yourself?
What are those statements? Write them down.
Challenge: Find Bible verses that deal with the
statement and write them next to each one.

_____

_____

_____

_____

_____

_____

_____

_____

_____

_____

_____

"There is no fear in love; but perfect love casts out fear, because fear involves torment. But he who fears has not been made perfect in love."

- 1 John 4:18 (NKJV)

12
Power over Paralysis

There was a time when I wondered if I'd ever get to the place where I could enjoy a normal day again. When anxiety showed up unannounced that day, my life was significantly altered ... for the better.

How did I get here? How is it possible that I have finally entered the world of bravery? The one where determination and faith meet up and make it possible to live a life worth living.

I got to this place by one heart wrenching, breathtaking step at a time.

When I was less than a year old, our Doctor told my parents that I needed a brace on my leg. My feet were turning in the wrong direction, and they needed to align them correctly. My family laughs at the way I handled this inconvenience. I refused to let it define or restrain me. That obnoxious brace was nothing but a small obstacle in my mind. At ten months, I learned to walk ... with a heavy cast trying to hold me back.

I've had different versions of that cast come up in my life since that time.

A terrorizing robbery at the age of eight which left me with invisible scars. Life-altering anxiety and depression which threatened to cripple me from the inside out. Misplaced empathy which left me drained and emotionally worn. Confusion over my purpose which led to ten years of aimless striving.

I think back to the moments when I couldn't even stand and have a regular conversation at church because my heart was beating so fast. Or the times I was held captive in my home, afraid that a trip to the store would send me into panic mode. I reflect on the days I wanted to stay in bed, rather than face the day and I'm amazed at how the grace of God has carried me.

If you had any idea just how much of a mess I have been, you wouldn't believe I could still move. You would wonder how I have been able to do anything I have accomplished. There were days I didn't think I could keep going, but through Christ's strength I did.

Most of the things I've done over the past decade have been by taking one beaten, bloody step at a time. I was terrified every single moment. And yet, here I am … by the grace of God. I have found that the power I needed to overcome my paralysis was in reach. It was through giving up my pride, asking for help, letting go of perfectionism, and falling into the arms of Jesus.

He made me whole. He used people, medicine, and the power of His Spirit. It hasn't always looked like I wanted it to, or played out the way I was comfortable with, but it has been an incredible journey. And, this journey isn't over.

I have come to understand the words of the Apostle Paul when he spoke about his thorn in the flesh. He said, "Concerning this thing I pleaded with the Lord three times that it might depart from me. And He said to me, "My grace is sufficient for you, for My strength is made perfect in weakness." Therefore most gladly I will rather boast in my infirmities, that the power of Christ may rest upon me. Therefore I take pleasure in infirmities, in reproaches, in needs, in persecutions, in distresses, for Christ's sake. For when I am weak, then I am strong." (II Corinthians 12:8-10 NKJV)

If I hadn't embarked on this life altering trek, I wouldn't know what God can do through weak, imperfect people. If I hadn't experienced the depth of emotions that accompany anxiety and depression, I wouldn't empathize with those who are suffering in the way that I do now. My eyes have been opened to a whole new world. There is suffering there. Raw pain. Real hurt. I see unresolved torment on the faces of so many people I meet and I want to tell them there is a better way.

We can learn to lean into God's goodness. We can trust His faithfulness. We can know that all things work together for good for those who love God and are called according to His purpose. (Romans 8:28 NASB). We can rest in His perfect love.

His love is without defect. It is perfect and it drives out fear. There was a time when I would read that verse and try to come up with ways to manufacture perfect love. I felt that if I could somehow get that kind of love that my fear would disappear. It took my some time to realize that I can't come up with perfect love, because I am imperfect. It is His love—and His love alone that can drive out our fear. The acceptance of His perfect love upon our damaged souls is the only thing that can lift the burdens off our shoulders. His love leads us away from striving and says "peace be still."

You can't create it. You can't manufacture it. Yet, so often we try to do just that. We look to people, jobs, positions, titles to fill us up. We incorrectly think that somehow if we fill our lives with the perfect things, that we will arrive at the place we want to be. It doesn't work that way.

It takes us walking with our own cast. That cumbersome thing in our lives that is trying to hold us down. It requires us to stare headlong at that inconvenience and say, "I don't care what you do to me, I'm not quitting." The most amazing truth that I have learned through all of this journey is that I don't walk alone. My Father wants to walk with me. As I courageously walk in this imperfect body, He gives me the strength to just keep moving.

We have a perfect God, who loves us in a perfect way. Say it to yourself until it settles deep within your being. "I have a perfect God, who loves me in a perfect way!" I don't have to figure everything out because the Creator of the Universe loves me and has a plan for my life. He is there to lead me to green pastures and He longs to restore my soul.

Even if you feel like you are a mess, remember you are being made into a beautiful masterpiece. As you surrender to God, you will be transformed into an incredible version of "you." Ask God to make you into the person that He thought of when He created you. His plans are better than the ones we come up with.

Let go of the things that are trying to hold you down.

Get up.

Walk forward, even if it is with a limp caused by your human experience. Walk in freedom, knowing that you have all the power you need. God's power gives victory over your paralysis.

Live free.

Find the bravery you need to walk one step at a time.

Journal Exercise

What is the "cast" in your life that is trying to hold you back?
What step do you need to take towards your freedom?

_____

_____

_____

_____

_____

_____

_____

_____

_____

_____

_____

_____

_____

"Take small steps every day and one day you will get there."

- Unknown

Afterword

I get choked up when I think about the word "freedom." The reason that word evokes emotions within me is because it has become a reality in my life. A reality I didn't think was possible.

I'm free. I'm not bound anymore by depression or anxiety. Even on days that are hard—days when I want to go back to bed, or I feel stirrings of fear within me, I realize with a glad heart that it doesn't control me. My feelings have become indicators, not dictators (as Lysa Terkeurst writes).

To be completely honest, there were so many days when I couldn't believe this day would come. I'm sure some of you are in the middle of bondage. You are probably feeling the chains wrapping around you so tightly that you feel you can't breathe. Let me assure you that God is your Deliverer. He will be your strength when you lean into His abundant goodness. It may take eleven years. It may take longer. You may experience years of fear and struggle and disappointment. You may feel like you are walking on a path to nowhere. Let me encourage you ... It's not over. Your story is just beginning.

I couldn't tell this story without telling you about the strong and mighty God who has my heart. I've been angry at Him during this process. I've cried out in frustration and fear. I've wondered how a God who loved me could allow me to go through something so horrible.

In those moments when life didn't feel worthy to be lived, He was there. He was that still, small voice reminding me to look up. To wait for my salvation. To be patient in my affliction. He helped me to see those around me who had endured. Those in history who had battled against impossible odds. He helped me see victory in my future when I couldn't humanly see it.

I needed to learn dependence on God. A kind of dependence that couldn't be shaken. I needed to understand that I couldn't do life on my own terms. I couldn't control every scenario. And it works out better when I don't even try to.

If I could convey one truth through this story, it would be the faithfulness of God. His faithful love is so remarkable that I can't even seem to find adequate words to describe its beauty. When I think of His faithfulness, I envision a suspension bridge. I see it stretching out over a jungle. It sways ... it rocks ... sometimes you think you might fall when you walk across the path. And yet, it's there. It's holding fast. And you are walking, one step at a time. Sometimes you trip. Sometimes you nearly fall. And the whole time, His faithful love is holding you up.

The day that I had to go to the emergency room for anxiety after I thought I was free was one of the most frustrating times I'd ever experienced. I cried the whole way to the hospital. I couldn't get my breath, and the tightness in my chest was overwhelming. And the entire time, all I could think was ... "I'm so embarrassed." I couldn't believe this was happening again. What had I done to deserve this? I thought I had done everything right. I had given it all to God, and here I was surrendering to my fear once again.

The following day I attended my class at Bible Study Fellowship. Wouldn't you know we had a special "community" time scheduled for that particular meeting. I didn't want to go. I didn't want to see people and be known by them. I felt so fake—smiling as if nothing was wrong.

I shoved fear aside and drove to the study. We sat in a circle for the fellowship time. Our leader asked us to share something about God and our relationship with Him. I tried to pretend that I didn't need to speak. I sat there, biting my lip, fighting away tears and wanting more than anything to be a different version of myself.

I finally gathered the courage to speak up.

"God and I are in a bit of a funk right now," I said. "I love Him. I will always choose Him, but I'm struggling with trusting Him." I gained strength as I saw compassion on the faces of the women around me. "I ended up in the ER this week with a panic attack. The very thing I've been free from knocked me down again. I've been sharing how good God has been for the past five months. I've been shouting about my freedom. And now I just feel stupid."

I saw a few ladies with tears in the corners of their eyes. I wondered if perhaps they too have had these moments of wondering. Of doubting.

They stopped and prayed for me ... right there ... on the spot. They invited God to be there for me and to continue to heal me. I'm grateful I didn't hide away in my home that day.

In the discussion that followed we were unpacking the idea of how trials can showcase the glory of God. How finding joy in the middle of the struggle can speak to who God is. I was struck by the idea that perhaps one of the reasons we must go through pain and turmoil is so that we can be reminded that we aren't home yet. This isn't real life ... it's only the precursor of the beautiful things to come.

We pray "May Your Kingdom come, May Your will be done on earth as it is in heaven," but do we realize the enormous chasm that exists between the two realities? This is our imperfect life. This is fallen creation. And we seek the face of Incarnate Deity to wipe away the tears that come from living this sometimes perplexing fate.

It's not that I don't think it's possible. He has lifted my head more times than I can count. He has come through in ways that shocked my socks off and shown me such an enormous amount of love that I was brought to my knees in humble reverence that the very breath of God would come to rest upon my tear-stained face.

I have seen God. I have not looked directly into His eyes or seen what His face looks like, but I have seen His heart. I know who He is. He is Light. He is Love. He is Living Bread. He reveals, and redeems and restores.

He is close to the brokenhearted. He truly is. I don't know that I would have known that to the extent that I do now.

I thought I would be healed completely. I imagined the chains would be gone and I would be able to do anything. I believed He could do that if He wanted to, but either He has not determined that should be my story, or I have not developed enough faith to claim my healing

Either way ... He is still good. He is still God and He is still good. I can stand on His promises and know they are true.

I can't rely on anything else to give me life. I need Him so desperately. Nothing can satisfy the longing I have in my heart. Nothing can fill it but Jesus. And I look to Him even now.

God,

You are my hope.

You are the only thing worth seeking.

I choose you.

I seek you.

I love you.

I will always choose you. No matter what. It's You and me, sweet Lord. You and me.

Thank you for always holding me. For whispering peace in the most terrifying moments.

I live for You alone and I pray that my life gives honor to Your name.

Acknowledgements

I will be forever grateful to my parents for the love and guidance they offered me during my childhood years. There aren't better people anywhere. I am brave today because of the way they lived their lives. Mom and Dad, thank you for being an example of fearlessness. I am blessed by the way you trust God.

Jen, you are not only a fabulous sister, but you also rock at editing my words. I couldn't have kept going without your support and encouragement. Jeremy, I am so thankful for your review and input.

To my extended family and friends, you have walked with me on this journey and been there for me when times were tough. I wish I would have let you in on my inner pain sooner. You've given me blessings I count often.

Bri, Bethany and Brittney, the three "B's" who have encouraged me to keep going when I've felt like quitting. You have been a lifeline to me through this journey.

Megan, Katie, Jack and Lauren, your Mom loves you more

than I could ever say. I can't believe I get a front row seat to see the amazing people you are every day. We are in this together.

Brian, I love you now more than ever. You have been a rock when my world was shifting. You have walked with me during the darkest of days ... and you stayed. Thank you for loving me and making me feel like I matter. I'll fight beside you any day. Let's get it done.

Jesus, You are everything. From that first time until now, it will always be You. Thank you for trusting me with this heartbreaking journey. Thank you for teaching me more through pain than I could have ever learned from ease. You knew what You were doing the whole time. God, You are still good.

Verses for Hope & Healing

The Lord is my light and my salvation;
Whom shall I fear?
The Lord is the strength of my life;
Of whom shall I be afraid?
Psalm 27:1 (NKJV)

So we can say with confidence,
"The Lord is my helper,
so I will have no fear.
What can mere people do to me?
Hebrews 13:6 (NLT)

In the multitude of my anxieties within me,
Your comforts delight my soul.
Psalm 94:19 (NKJV)

The Lord is for me, so I will have no fear.
What can mere people do to me?
Psalm 118:6 (NLT)

God is our refuge and strength,
A very present help in trouble.
Psalm 46:1 (NKJV)

For God has not given us a spirit
of fear, but of power and of
love and of a sound mind.
II Timothy 1:7 (NKJV)

"So be strong and courageous! Do not be afraid and do not
panic before them. For the Lord your God will personally go
ahead of you. He will neither fail you nor abandon you."
Deuteronomy 31:6 (NLT)

"Give your burdens to the Lord,
and he will take care of you.
He will not permit the godly to slip and fall."
Psalm 55:22 (NLT)

"Have I not commanded you? Be strong and of
good courage; do not be afraid, nor be dismayed, for
the Lord your God is with you wherever you go."
Joshua 1:9 (NKJV)

But now, thus says the Lord, who created you, O Jacob,
And He who formed you, O Israel:
"Fear not, for I have redeemed you;
I have called you by your name;
Isaiah 43:1 (NKJV)

"The Lord your God in your midst, The Mighty One, will
save; He will rejoice over you with gladness, He will quiet
you with His love, He will rejoice over you with singing."
Zephaniah 3:17 (NKJV)

"You must not fear them,
For the LORD your God Himself fights for you"
Deuteronomy 3:22 (NKJV)

"I prayed to the Lord, and he answered me.
He freed me from all of my fears."
Psalm 34:4 (NLT)

Resources

www.focusonthefamily.com/lifechallenges/christian-counselors
-network

http://www.aacc.net/

https://spiritualgiftstest.com/

https://www.gallupstrengthscenter.com/home/en-us/Index

Printed in the United States
By Bookmasters